Series / Number 0

NONRECURSIVE CAUSAL MODELS

WILLIAM D. BERRY
Florida State University

SAGE PUBLICATIONS
The International Professional Publishers
Newbury Park   London   New Delhi

For information address:

SAGE Publications, Inc.
2455 Teller Road
Newbury Park, California 91320

SAGE Publications Ltd.
6 Bonhill Street
London EC2A 4PU
United Kingdom

SAGE Publications India Pvt. Ltd.
M-32 Market
Greater Kailash I
New Delhi 110 048 India

International Standard Book Number 0-8039-2265-5

Library of Congress Catalog Card No. 83-051542

93 94 10 9 8 7

When citing a professional paper, please use the proper form. Remember to cite the correct Sage University Paper series title and include the paper number. One of the following formats can be adapted (depending on the style manual used):

(1) IVERSEN, GUDMUND R. and NORPOTH, HELMUT (1976) "Analysis of Variance." Sage University Paper series on Quantitative Applications in the Social Sciences, 07-001. Beverly Hills and London: Sage Pubns.

OR

(2) Iversen, Gudmund R. and Norpoth, Helmut, 1976. *Analysis of Variance.* Sage University Paper series on Quantitative Applications in the Social Sciences, series no. 07-001. Beverly Hills and London: Sage Pubns.

CONTENTS

Series Editor's Introduction

As theories in the social sciences become more complex, the simplest statistical models need to be supplemented by ones that mirror this complexity. So it is with regression models, in which research has increasingly moved beyond single-equation models to multiequation models. Sometimes the latter are themselves relatively simple—as when causal effects are thought to be "unidirectional," permitting the use of so-called recursive models. Often, however, a presumption of unidirectionality is unrealistic, so analysts move on to nonrecursive models.

As these developments take place, the need expands for well-written and reasonably thorough yet introductory discussions of the more complex techniques. What becomes especially important is that such volumes convey a real understanding of the procedures—their uses, the assumptions on which they are based, the interpretation of the results, and so on. Such a volume is William Berry's *Nonrecursive Causal Models*.

Berry assumes that the reader has a passing familiarity with recursive causal models, at the level, for example, of Herbert Asher's *Causal Modeling*, an earlier paper in this series. To refresh readers' memories and to build an appropriate bridge, Berry briefly reviews the assumptions of such models in Chapter 1 and then goes on to show how nonrecursive models can be used to estimate more complex systems of equations.

Much of the rest of the volume focuses on the "identification" problem. Since identifying systems of equations is typically the most difficult research task, the effort to convey this material as clearly as possible is an important component of the book. As a further advantage in an introductory volume, Berry explains this material in a way that does not require knowledge of matrix algebra.

Finally, in the last chapter, Berry reviews common techniques for estimating parameters of nonrecursive models that are identified. Throughout, a series of examples is used from economics, political science, and sociology.

5

Because of its clear exposition of a complex technique, *Nonrecursive Causal Models* is a welcome new addition to our series of papers on methodology in the social sciences.

—Richard G. Niemi
Series Co-Editor

Acknowledgments

I would like to thank Frances Stokes Berry, and the co-editor of this series, Richard Niemi, for their careful reviews of this paper. Thanks also go to John Sullivan who, by giving me a sound background in quantitative methods in my first graduate seminar on the subject, made a very important indirect contribution to the manuscript. Finally, I am grateful to many at the University of Kentucky who helped in the preparation of this monograph. In particular, Bradley Miller spent considerable time working at a computer terminal developing illustrations, and Kim Hayden spent even more time typing the monograph. Also, I wish to acknowledge the efforts of the students in my 1983 research methods graduate seminar in uncovering several errors in an earlier version of this paper.

–William D. Berry

NONRECURSIVE CAUSAL MODELS

WILLIAM D. BERRY
Florida State University

1. INTRODUCTION

The most common strategy in empirical social science research involves specifying a single-equation model and then estimating the coefficients for the equation using data from a sample of cases; one variable is conceptualized as the *dependent* variable, and is assumed to be influenced by one or more *explanatory* (or *independent*) variables. For example, one might develop a single-equation model about voting behavior in elections that suggests that an individual's comparative evaluation of the opposing candidates in a given election is a dependent variable determined by two explanatory variables—(1) an individual's policy or issue positions [X_1], and (2) an individual's political party identification [X_2]—plus an error term:[1]

$$\text{Candidate Evaluation} = a + b_1 X_1 + b_2 X_2 + e \qquad [1]$$

Then, if we were given data for the three variables for a sample of cases, and if we were willing to make the specific set of assumptions about the model necessary for regression analysis (see Lewis-Beck, 1980), we could use ordinary least squares (OLS) regression analysis to estimate the coefficients—a, b_1, and b_2—for the equation. Then the coefficient estimate for an explanatory variable could be interpreted as an estimate of the direct effect of that variable on the dependent variable (comparative candidate evaluation) where the value of the other explanatory variable is held constant. For example, the estimate of b_1 would represent the direct effect of policy or issue positions on candidate evaluations, assuming that the value of party identification is held constant.

But many social science theories suggest causal relationships among variables that are too complex to be reflected in a single-equation model.[2] For example, in a model in which a dependent variable is

7

assumed to be influenced by several explanatory variables, the theory underlying the model might suggest that some of the explanatory variables are causes of one another. For instance, in the case of voting behavior, we might modify the single-equation model of equation 1 by recognizing that an individual's policy/issue positions is a variable that likely influences party identification (party ID); this expectation might be based on a belief that people adopting an affiliation with a political party are guided—at least partially—by the issue stances and general ideological position of the leaders and candidates of the party with which they identify. When added to the earlier model, this hypothesis generates a model suggesting causal relationships specified schematically in the diagram in Figure 1.[3] The model suggests that party identification and policy/issue positions are both factors that determine candidate evaluation, but that policy/issue positions also have a direct effect on an individual's party identification. In a sense, then, policy/issue positions are thought to affect candidate evaluation both directly (as in the earlier model of equation 1), and indirectly (through its effect on party ID). The theory of candidate choice represented in Figure 1 cannot be modeled using only one equation; instead, a *multiequation* model is needed.

Indeed, multiequation (or causal) models have been used with increasing frequency in social science research, and with highly fruitful results. Many social scientists are probably most familiar with a narrow subset of multiequation models referred to as *recursive* causal models. Recursive causal models have been used often by sociologists and political scientists over the last two decades (see Land, 1969; Duncan et al., 1971). To be recursive, a model must satisfy several conditions that together ensure that all causal effects specified in the model are "unidirectional" in nature, i.e., that no two variables in the model are reciprocally related, with each affecting the other. Also, all pairs of error (or disturbance) terms in the model must be assumed to be uncorrelated. An advantage of recursive models is the ease with which the coefficients for such models can be estimated. All recursive models are "identified." While the precise meaning of the term "identified" will not be presented until the next chapter, we can note now that, in order for it to be possible to determine estimates for the coefficients of a multiequation model that give meaningful information about the nature of causal effects, the model must first be identified. Furthermore, the assumptions made in recursive models permit one to use OLS regression analysis to obtain unbiased estimates of the model's coefficients.[4] Thus, social scientists trained in regression analysis can move into analysis of recursive models with little difficulty.

However, the assumptions made in recursive models are often at odds with our understanding of the nature of the social science process being studied. In many cases it is unrealistic to assume that no two variables in

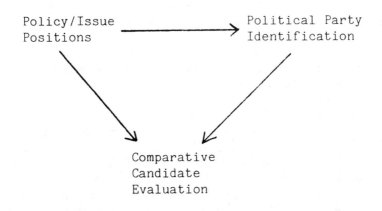

Figure 1: A Schematic "Causal Diagram" Suggesting Causal Relationships Among Variables: A Voting Behavior Example

a model are reciprocally related; furthermore, given our generally high degree of ignorance about the factors represented in a model's disturbance terms, it is often impossible to provide a convincing justification for an assumption that each error term in a model is uncorrelated with all other error terms in the model. In such cases, we must abandon recursive models, and employ *nonrecursive* multiequation (or simultaneous equation) models. These models allow for both patterns of reciprocal causation among variables and assumptions that one or more pairs of error terms in the model have nonzero correlations.

Nonrecursive models have been widely used in economics for several decades and, thus, are a core topic in nearly all econometrics textbooks (e.g., Klein, 1962; Christ, 1966; Theil, 1971). But political scientists and sociologists have employed nonrecursive models far less frequently. Some exceptions are studies by political scientists Hibbs (1973), Jackson (1975), and Erikson (1976), and sociologists Mason and Halter (1968), Land (1971), and Waite and Stolzenberg (1976). This infrequency is probably because the use of nonrecursive models opens up research problems not present with recursive models. For example, some nonrecursive models are "nonidentified." While we will delay a formal definition of this term until the next chapter, it turns out that with nonidentified models, it is impossible to determine meaningful coefficient estimates for the model, even when supplied with the best possible data.

The meaning of "identification" and an analysis of what causes some nonrecursive models to be "nonidentified" will be the subject of Chapter 2 of this book. Fortunately, some simple tests to determine whether or not a model is identified are available; these tests will be presented in Chapters 3 and 4. In Chapter 5 I will discuss strategies for modifying nonidentified models to bring about identification. Then, in Chapter 6, I will present procedures appropriate for estimating the coefficients of an identified nonrecursive model. It turns out that OLS regression—which is suitable for recursive causal models—is inappropriate with nonrecursive models. Fortunately, however, we can modify OLS regression to obtain procedures that will give consistent coefficient estimates for nonrecursive models.[5]

Most detailed discussions of nonrecursive simultaneous equation models require an understanding of matrix algebra. This is because the best technique for testing whether a model is identified—the rank condition—has traditionally been presented in a form that requires analysis using matrix algebra. However, this book presents an algorithm that allows one to use the rank condition without having had previous exposure to matrix algebra. While no knowledge of matrix algebra is required, this book does assume a knowledge of OLS regression analysis, and a general familiarity with recursive causal models.[6]

Definitions and Notation

An analysis of multiequation models requires the definition of some important terms, and the development of some notation for presenting such models. First, we must distinguish between several types of variables found in multiequation models. *Endogenous* variables are those the causes of which are explicitly represented in the model. Thus, they are variables that the theory underlying the model attempts to explain.

In contrast, *predetermined* variables are variables the causes of which are *not* explicitly represented in the model. Put differently, these variables have values assumed to be determined outside of the model; they are, thus, treated as givens that the model's theory does not explain.[7] We can further distinguish two types of variables treated as predetermined. The first, *lagged endogenous* variables, have values equal to the values of endogenous variables in the model at previous points in time. The second, *exogenous* variables, have values determined completely outside of the model and are not simply prior values of endogenous variables. Since in most social science research, all predetermined variables used are exogenous, I will, on most occasions, distinguish simply between exogenous and endogenous variables. However, any time I employ the term "exogenous" variable, I am referring, more precisely, to the broader class of predetermined variables.[8]

Throughout the book I will denote endogenous variables using X's— letting $X_1, X_2, \ldots, X_m$ denote a set of m endogenous variables in a model (where, since we have a multiequation model, $m \geq 2$). Z's, on the other hand, will be used to represent exogenous variables so that $Z_{m+1}, Z_{m+2}, \ldots,$ Z_{m+k} denote the k exogenous variables in a model (where $k \geq 1$). Given this notation, a simultaneous equation model that views each of the m endogenous variables in a model as directly influenced by all the other variables in the model is usually referred to as a *full nonrecursive* model, and can be expressed by a system of m *structural equations*, each expressing an endogenous variable X_i in terms of all the variables in the model assumed to have direct causal effects on X_i:[9]

$$X_1 = \beta_{12}X_2 + \cdots\cdots\cdots\cdots + \beta_{1m}X_m + \gamma_{1,m+1}Z_{m+1} + \cdots + \gamma_{1,m+k}Z_{m+k} + \epsilon_1$$

$$X_2 = \beta_{21}X_1 + \cdots\cdots\cdots\cdots + \beta_{2m}X_m + \gamma_{2,m+1}Z_{m+1} + \cdots + \gamma_{2,m+k}Z_{m+k} + \epsilon_2$$

$$\vdots$$

$$X_m = \beta_{m1}X_1 + \beta_{m2}X_2 + \cdots + \beta_{m,m-1}X_{m-1} \qquad + \gamma_{m,m+1}Z_{m+1} + \cdots + \gamma_{m,m+k}Z_{m+k} + \epsilon_m \quad [2]$$

In these structural equations, β_{ij} denotes the coefficient or parameter representing the direct effect of the endogenous variable X_j on the endogenous variable X_i—in particular, the amount of change in X_i that would result if X_j were increased one unit, while all other variables in the model were held constant. γ_{ij}, in turn, represents the direct effect of exogenous variable Z_j on endogenous variable X_i—the amount of change in X_i resulting from a unit change in Z_j, with all other variables held constant. Finally, the term ϵ_i in the structural equation defining X_i is an error (or disturbance) term, which represents the effects of all other variables not explicitly included in the model on the endogenous variable X_i.

Recursive Causal Models:
A Brief Review

By making some very strict assumptions about the nature of the parameters and error terms in the full nonrecursive model of equation system 2, we can develop a recursive causal model. A model is called "recursive" if several conditions are met.

First, the model must be *hierarchical*. A model is hierarchical if all endogenous variables in the model can be arranged and labeled in a sequence $X_1, X_2, \ldots, X_m$ such that for any X_i and X_j where $i < j$, X_j cannot be viewed as a cause of X_i; therefore, β_{ij} must be equal to zero. Thus, the endogenous variables in the model must be subject to being ordered so that the first endogenous variable is determined only by exogenous variables; the second is influenced only by exogenous variables and the first endogenous variable; the third is influenced by exogenous variables and the first and second endogenous variables; and so on. Consequently, in a recursive model, no two endogenous variables can be viewed as reciprocally related with each being a direct cause of the other. Also, there must be no indirect causal linkages which result in any endogenous variable's affecting an endogenous variable before it in the causal ordering. Finally, in addition to being hierarchical, all recursive models assume that each error term is uncorrelated with (1) all exogenous variables, and (2) all other error terms in the model. In notational form, cov (ϵ_i, ϵ_j) must equal 0 for all values of i and j between 1 and m, and cov (ϵ_i, Z_j) must equal zero for all values of i between 1 and m, and all values of j between m+1 and m+k.

It can be shown that the assumptions of a recursive model together imply that—when the endogenous variables are labeled in hierarchical order $X_1, X_2, \ldots, X_m$—cov $(X_i, \epsilon_j) = 0$ for all i $< $ j (Namboodiri et al., 1975: 444-448; Duncan, 1975: Chap. 4). Thus, the error term for a given equation, say ϵ_j, will necessarily be uncorrelated with endogenous variables $X_1, X_2, \ldots, X_{j-1}$. But since each error term is uncorrelated with all exogenous variables in the model (by an earlier assumption), ϵ_j will be uncorrelated with *all* explanatory variables in the equation containing ϵ_j. It is this feature of recursive models which allows researchers to employ OLS regression analysis to estimate the coefficients of a recursive model and obtain estimators that are unbiased and consistent.[10] Thus, recursive models have the advantage of ease of estimation of parameters; we can deal with them using the same tools that we use with single-equation regression models.

But in many situations the assumptions of recursive models are unrealistic. Consider the model of voting behavior represented schematically in Figure 1. This model can be formally expressed as a recursive model with the following equations:

$$X_1 = \gamma_{13}Z_3 + \epsilon_1 \qquad [3]$$

$$X_2 = \beta_{21}X_1 + \gamma_{23}Z_3 + \epsilon_2 \qquad [4]$$

where Z_3 represents the individual's policy/issue positions—the single exogenous variable in the model—and where there are two endogenous variables: the party ID of the individual (denoted X_1) and the individual's comparative candidate evaluation (denoted X_2). Note that our model satisfies the condition that recursive models be hierarchical; the two endogenous variables can be ordered "X_1, X_2" where X_1 (Party ID) is determined only by the exogenous variable Z_3, and where X_2 (Candidate Evaluation) is influenced only by Z_3 and X_1. Since the model is to be recursive, we must assume that cov $(\epsilon_1, \epsilon_2) = 0$, and that both error terms are uncorrelated with exogenous variable Z_3.[11] This recursive model can be represented schematically by the causal diagram in Figure 2.

But many would argue that the assumptions required for a recursive model are not justified in this situation. First, the hierarchical nature of the model can be questioned. For example, while party ID may influence the individual's comparative evaluation of the candidates in an election, the candidate evaluations may in turn modify attitudes about the parties the candidates represent, and thus the individual's party identification. We could also question the assumption of the model that neither comparative candidate evaluation nor party ID affects policy/issue positions. It is possible that when formulating positions on issues, citizens take cues from the political leaders and parties they support. If this were the case, we would have to allow for the possibility that both comparative candidate evaluation and political party ID have direct effects on policy/issue positions. Given these hypotheses, our voting behavior model would no longer be hierarchical. In fact, with a revised model taking into account the additional hypothesized causal effects, policy/issue positions would become endogenous, and each of the endogenous variables in the model would be viewed as a cause of all other endogenous variables, as reflected schematically in Figure 3.

One could also question whether the assumptions about error terms required for a recursive model are reasonable for the model of Figure 2. I noted earlier that an error term can be conceived as representing the effects of variables not explicitly included in a model. Given this conception, consider the assumption that ϵ_1 and ϵ_2 are uncorrelated. For this assumption to be reasonable, we must believe that the factors that influence an individual's party ID but have not been explicitly brought into the model are uncorrelated with the factors that influence an individual's candidate evaluation but are not explicitly in the model. Similarly, to accept the assumption that the error terms are uncorrelated with the exogenous variable Z_3, we must believe that the "omitted factors" reflected by the error terms are uncorrelated with the individual's policy/issue positions.

Page and Jones (1979) propose a model of voting behavior in presidential elections that contains the three variables in the recursive model of Figure 2. But Page and Jones's model includes a variable specifically hypothesized to influence both the individual's (current) party identification and his/her comparative presidential candidate evaluation: the individual's "partisan voting history," i.e., the degree of consistency in the individual's support for a single party in previous presidential elections. If Page and Jones are correct, then partisan voting history is a factor reflected in the error terms for both X_1 (Party ID) and X_2 (Candidate Evaluation) in the model of Figure 2; consequently, we can expect ϵ_1 and ϵ_2 to be correlated, thus making the assumptions of a recursive model inappropriate. Page and Jones also propose that two variables—(1) education, and (2) ideology (measured on a left-right

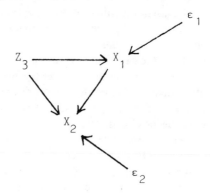

Assumptions: $\quad \mathrm{cov}(\varepsilon_1,\varepsilon_2) = \mathrm{cov}(\varepsilon_1,Z_3) = \mathrm{cov}(\varepsilon_2,Z_3) = 0$

Notation: $\quad\quad X_1$ -- Political Party ID

$\quad\quad\quad\quad\quad X_2$ -- Comparative Candidate Evaluation

$\quad\quad\quad\quad\quad Z_3$ -- Policy/Issue Positions

Figure 2: A Causal Diagram of the Model of Equations 3 and 4

continuum)—have direct effects on both party ID and policy/issue positions. If this is correct, then the assumption of our recursive model that the error term ε_1 in equation 3 is uncorrelated with the model's exogenous variable, Z_3 (policy/issue positions), is unjustified.

Error terms can be correlated with one another not only when theoretically important variables are omitted from a model, but also as a result of measurement error. Unless the measurement of the variables in a model is perfect, measurement error constitutes one component of the error terms in the model. To the extent that similar measuring devices are used to measure several endogenous variables in a model, any systematic errors produced by the measuring device will tend to be present in a similar fashion in each of the variables, thus resulting in correlated error terms. For example, if the variables in the model of voting behavior in Figure 2 were operationalized using data collected on the same survey, it is possible that (1) similarities in the phrasing of questions used to measure several variables, (2) the nature of the interviewer, (3) similar errors in the coding of responses from question to question, and (4) other survey characteristics could result in the error terms for the equations being mutually correlated.

If we were to accept any of these challenges to the assumptions of the recursive model of voting behavior in Figure 2, and thus relax the assumptions of the model so that they were more realistic, the model would cease to be recursive, and indeed, in this case the model would no longer be identified. Consequently, meaningful estimates for the parameters of the model could not be obtained.

In sum, there is often considerable reason for doubting that the strict assumptions required for a recursive model are appropriate. Therefore, the decision to use a recursive model should not be taken lightly, or simply for the purpose of convenience. Unless one is convinced that (1) causation among the variables is strictly unidirectional and (2) the factors constituting the error terms in the model are fundamentally different for each equation, recursive models should not be used. Instead, efforts should be directed toward developing more realistic nonrecursive models. If a recursive model is employed when the assumptions required are violated and if OLS regression is used to estimate the coefficients of the model, the resulting estimates will be biased and inconsistent and, thus, will give an inaccurate assessment of the nature of the magnitude of causal effects.

Nonrecursive Models: Some Assumptions

I present in equation system 2 the *full nonrecursive* model for m endogenous variables and k exogenous variables. In a full nonrecursive model, each endogenous variable is assumed to be directly affected by all other endogenous and exogenous variables in the model. For example, we could develop a full nonrecursive vote choice model that reflects the causal relationships represented schematically in Figure 3, plus the effects of a single exogenous variable—level of education—on the endogenous variables in the model. If we were cautious we would develop the model assuming that education—to be denoted by Z_4—has a direct impact on all three endogenous variables. This would produce the model depicted in the arrow diagram in Figure 4 (in which the dotted-line arrow is to be read as a normal arrow), and represented by the following equations:

$$X_1 = \beta_{12}X_2 + \beta_{13}X_3 + \gamma_{14}Z_4 + \epsilon_1 \tag{5}$$

$$X_2 = \beta_{21}X_1 + \beta_{23}X_3 + \gamma_{24}Z_4 + \epsilon_2 \tag{6}$$

$$X_3 = \beta_{31}X_1 + \beta_{32}X_2 + \gamma_{34}Z_4 + \epsilon_3 \tag{7}$$

However, to be useful in empirical research, a nonrecursive model cannot be *full* nonrecursive, for such models—as we shall see below—

16

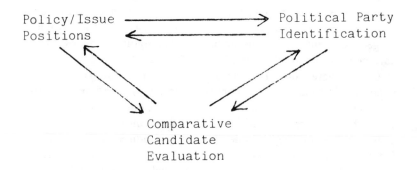

Figure 3: A Schematic Causal Diagram Suggesting Reciprocal Causation Among Variables: A Voting Behavior Example

are not identified. Instead, typically, some of the parameters of a non-recursive model are assumed to be equal to zero. This means substantively that some variables are assumed not to have direct causal impacts on one or more endogenous variables in the model. For example, Page and Jones (1979) assume that education has no direct effect on candidate evaluations, and that any effect of education on candidate evaluations is indirect through education's effect on policy/issue positions and party ID. If we accept this assumption, we could develop a new model that is not full by assuming that $\gamma_{24} = 0$. This would result in the model represented by the arrow diagram in Figure 4 with the dotted-line arrow *deleted*, and the equation system including equations 5 and 7, but with equation 6 replaced by the following equation:

$$X_2 = \beta_{21}X_1 + \beta_{23}X_3 + \epsilon_2 \qquad [6']$$

An alert reader may have noted that we have not yet made any assumptions about the error terms in the model of equation system 2, or in the nonrecursive model of vote choice just examined. Thus, we must make some explicit assumptions. And, indeed, the nature of these assumptions will greatly influence whether or not a model is identified. In this paper we will restrict our attention (except in Appendix 2) to nonrecursive models making the following typical assumptions:

(1) $cov(\epsilon_i, Z_j) = 0$ for all i and j (i.e., each error term in a model is uncorrelated with all exogenous variables in the model), and

(2) $E(X_i) = E(Z_i) = E(\epsilon_i) = 0$ for all i (i.e., all variables and error terms have a mean of zero).

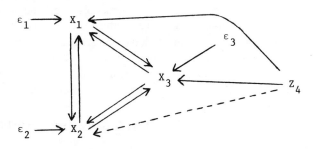

Assumptions: cov(ε₁,Z₄) = cov(ε₂,Z₄) = cov(ε₃,Z₄) = 0

Notation:
X₁ -- Political Party ID
X₂ -- Comparative Candidate Evaluation
X₃ -- Policy/Issue Positions
X₄ -- Education

Assumptions: $\quad \text{cov}(\varepsilon_1, Z_4) = \text{cov}(\varepsilon_2, Z_4) = \text{cov}(\varepsilon_3, Z_4) = 0$

Notation:
X_1 -- Political Party ID

X_2 -- Comparative Candidate Evaluation

X_3 -- Policy/Issue Positions

X_4 -- Education

Figure 4: A Causal Diagram of the Full Nonrecursive Model of Equations 5, 6, and 7

We make assumption 2 for ease of presentation. It is merely a convention as to the location of the origin of the measurement scales for variables, which permits us to delete constant terms from a model's equations.

On the other hand, assumption 1 is very important; it has a significant impact on whether or not a nonrecursive model will be identified. Indeed, while the assumption is reasonable in many substantive situations, if one is unwilling to make it for a particular model, the test for identification presented in this paper is not necessarily applicable. On the other hand, in some situations one might be prepared to make an assumption about error terms stronger than assumption 1. For example, in addition to assuming that each error term is uncorrelated with all exogenous variables in the model, one may be willing to assume that some error terms are uncorrelated with one another. In such a case, the test for identification presented will also not be applicable (without modification). See Appendix 2 for a discussion of one class of nonrecursive models, called block recursive models, which assume that some pairs of error terms are uncorrelated.

Note, however, that it would not make sense to assume that each error term is uncorrelated with all endogenous variables in a nonrecursive model; for in such models, at least one error term is bound to be correlated with one or more endogenous variables in the model. For example, in the model represented in Figure 4 and by equations 5, 6, and 7, it would make no sense to assume that ϵ_3 is uncorrelated with X_2. This is because ϵ_3 is assumed to have a direct causal effect on X_3, which in turn is assumed to have a direct impact on X_2. Thus, the model specifically establishes ϵ_3 as an indirect cause of X_2 (through X_3); consequently $cov(\epsilon_3, X_2)$ cannot be assumed to be equal to zero.

2. THE IDENTIFICATION PROBLEM

We noted in Chapter 1 that all recursive models are identified, and thus satisfy a key necessary condition for being able to obtain meaningful parameter estimates. If all recursive models are identified, what goes "wrong" with some nonrecursive models to make them nonidentified? Intuitively, it may seem that if good and ample data for a model were available, we should always be able to determine the model's parameters. But a look at the simplest of nonidentified models suggests why this intuition is misleading. Consider the model diagramed below and expressed by the following equations:

$$X_1 = \beta_{12} X_2 + \epsilon_1 \tag{8}$$

$$X_2 = \beta_{21} X_1 + \epsilon_2 \tag{9}$$

This model is not identified. And in this model, the failure to be identified essentially reduces to the widely recognized impossibility of inferring the direction of causation between two variables X_1 and X_2 simply by knowing their relationship (e.g., their correlation) at a single point in time. By allowing for reciprocal causation between the variables, we must not simply determine a single parameter expressing the strength of the relationship between X_1 and X_2; we must also sort out what "part" of the relationship goes in one causal direction and what part in the other. In more complex nonrecursive models, a similar problem can occur. In particular, in a nonrecursive model there are often more parameters to be determined than in a recursive model including the same variables; in addition, the researcher often has *less information* to work with in a nonrecursive model than in a recursive model, since the assumption that all pairs of error terms are uncorrelated is not made.

A Supply and Demand Example

To understand the meaning of identification, it is useful to begin by looking at an illustrative model involving the concepts of supply and demand from economics. Indeed, a discussion of the requirements for identifying the parameters of a supply curve and a demand curve is the most commonly used vehicle for introducing the notion of identification.

Consider first the *demand curve* for some agricultural commodity, say wheat. The demand curve shows the total amount of wheat consumers are willing to purchase at any given price. We will assume that consumer behavior is sufficiently similar over the period of analysis to justify an assumption that the demand curve is stable over time. To simplify the analysis, we will also assume that the demand curve is linear and thus can be expressed by the following equation:

$$\text{Demand Curve:} \qquad D_t = a_D + b_D P_t \qquad [10]$$

where D_t represents the quantity of wheat consumers are willing to purchase at time t, P_t denotes the price for a unit of wheat during the same period, and a_D and b_D are parameters (intercept and slope, respectively) assumed to be constant over time. We can help narrow down the value of the slope coefficient by hypothesizing—as is typical—that the quantity consumers are willing to purchase is negatively related to price, and thus assuming that $b_D < 0$. Given this assumption, we know that the demand curve slopes in the typical downward direction as in the graph in Figure 5. If it were possible to observe D_t—the quantity of wheat consumers are willing to purchase—at two different prices (say P_1 and P_2 in Figure 5), we would then know the positions of two points that lie on the demand curve (points 1 and 2). And since two points determine a line, we would know the position of the line in Figure 5, and thus the value of the demand curve parameters a_D and b_D.

But, of course, we must bring a *supply curve* into the model of the wheat market. The supply curve shows the total amount of wheat that producers are willing to put on the market at any given price. As with the demand curve, we will assume that the supply curve is linear and stable over the period of analysis. Thus, it can be expressed by the following equation:

$$\text{Supply Curve:} \qquad S_t = a_S + b_S P_t \qquad [11]$$

where S_t represents the quantity of wheat that producers are willing to sell at time t, and where a_S and b_S are parameters assumed to remain constant over time. It is reasonable to assume that price and the quantity producers are willing to supply would be positively related; thus, we restrict the slope coefficient b_s to be greater than zero. Similar to the case of the demand curve, if we were able to observe the quantity that producers were willing to supply at two or more prices, we would be able to pinpoint the positions of at least 2 points on the supply curve, and therefore, the parameters of the supply curve—b_S and a_S—would be determined.

In the real world, however, we can observe neither the quantity that consumers would be willing to purchase nor the amount that producers would be willing to sell at multiple prices. In the real world we can observe these quantities for only *one* price—namely, the price for which the amount farmers are willing to sell is equal to the amount consumers are willing to purchase, i.e., the price for which $S_t = D_t$. Since at this price, S_t does equal D_t, we can let $S_t = D_t = Q_t$, where Q_t represents the amount of wheat sold at time t. Thus, we can rewrite the equations for the demand and supply curve (10 and 11 respectively) as:

Demand Curve: $\qquad Q_t = a_D + b_D P_t \qquad\qquad$ [10']

Supply Curve: $\qquad Q_t = a_S + b_S P_t \qquad\qquad$ [11']

So, in the real world we can observe that at wheat's actual price, p_o, some amount, q_o, of the commodity is sold. This observation allows us to locate point 1 on the graph in Figure 6; but we do not have sufficient information to locate any other points on either the supply or demand curves. While we know that the demand curve and the supply curve both go through point 1, we have no knowledge about the parameters of the demand or supply curves beyond our assumption that $b_D < 0$ and $b_S > 0$. For example, our observation is consistent with both (1) the hypothesis that the supply curve is S' and the demand curve is D', and (2) the hypothesis that the supply curve is S" and the demand curve is D". Consequently, the positions of the demand and supply curves have not been revealed; thus, the parameters of equations 10' and 11' are not determined. In this situation, we would say that equations 10' and 11' are not identified, as our observation is consistent with more than 1 set of parameters for the model.[12]

Suppose we believe that the supply curve for wheat shifts over time, while the demand curve (as before) remains stable. For example, we may believe that the amount of rainfall in a time period is an exogenous variable that affects the position of the supply curve but not the demand curve. For any fixed price, as the amount of rainfall increases, we can

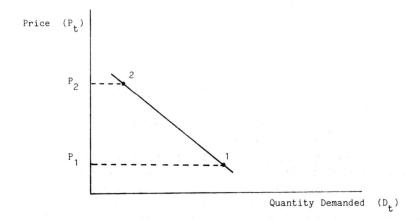

Figure 5: Demand Curve of Equation 10

expect crop yields to increase, thus leading to a reduction in the cost per unit of wheat grown. A decrease in the cost of growing wheat, in turn, can be expected to increase the amount of wheat that farmers would be willing to supply at the given price. In contrast, it is reasonable to assume that the amount of rainfall in a period does not directly influence the amount of wheat consumers are willing to purchase at a given price.

This new expectation about the relationship between rainfall and the quantity producers are willing to sell can be reflected in the following revised supply equation:

$$\text{Supply Surface:} \quad Q_t = a_S + b_S P_t + b_R R_t \qquad [12]$$

where R_t represents the amount of rainfall in time period t, and the parameter b_R is assumed to be greater than zero. Since the supply equation now includes three variables, it cannot be adequately represented by a graph in two dimensions, as it is really a supply *surface* in three-dimensional space. The graph in Figure 7 depicts this supply surface (denoted S) by presenting its level-curves for several values of rainfall: r_1, r_2, r_3, and r_4. Each level-curve of the supply *surface* can be thought of as a supply *curve*—describing the relationship between price and the quantity that producers are willing to sell—associated with a specific amount of rainfall. In the graph, as rainfall increases from r_1 to r_2 to r_3 to r_4, the level-curve for the surface supply shifts downward and to the right. (Note that the slope of the shifting supply level-curve in the graph was arbitrarily chosen, since, while the slope of the level-curve remains the same regardless of rainfall amount, the value of the slope is unknown.) But while the supply level-curve shifts depending on the

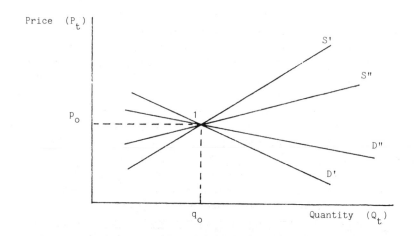

Figure 6: Demand and Supply Curves of Equations 10′ and 11′

amount of rainfall, the demand curve, D, remains at a fixed position. As a consequence, the intersection of the fixed demand curve with the shifting supply level-curve traces out a line. But all the points on this line are on the demand curve; so the line traced out is precisely the demand curve. So, if we were to observe the price of wheat, and the amount of wheat sold at that price, for at least two different amounts of rainfall, at least two points on the demand curve, D, would be defined. This in turn would permit us to determine the slope and intercept of the demand curve and, thus, the parameters a_D and b_D in equation 10′. Thus, the introduction of the exogeneous variable, amount of rainfall, into the model makes the demand curve (equation 10′) identified, as knowledge of the price of wheat and the amount sold overtime would determine the parameters of the equation.

But knowledge of the price of the commodity and the amount sold at different points in time (and thus different levels of rainfall) would not help us determine the parameters of the supply surface. For example, we still do not know the slope of the level-curves for the surface, as the observed pattern of price and quantity sold over time would be consistent with any positive value for b_S in equation 12. For this reason, we would say that equation 12 is not identified.

If we were to expand our market model by assuming that per capita disposable income is an exogenous variable that influences the amount of wheat consumers are willing to purchase, but *not* the amount producers are willing to supply, we could hypothesize that the demand equation takes the following form:

Demand Surface: $\quad D_t = a_D + b_D P_t + b_I I_t$ [13]

where I_t denotes per capita disposable income at time t, and where the parameter b_1 is assumed to be positive. Analysis of this equation similar to the above would show that the introduction of I_t in the model's demand equation serves to identify the supply surface. The level-curve for the demand surface shifts over time depending upon the level of disposable income and, thus, traces out points on the supply surface. Thus, if we could observe the price of wheat and the amount sold at two or more levels of income, we would have sufficient information to determine the parameters of the supply surface.

This example illustrates that making stronger assumptions about the factors affecting the amount of wheat consumers are willing to purchase (D_t) and the amount producers are willing to sell (S_t) served to identify the equations in the wheat market model. In its original form (equations 10 and 11), no amount of observation of the relationship between the price of wheat and the quantity sold would give us information sufficient to determine the parameters of the model's equations. While further observation would not help us, further assumptions about the factors affecting D_t and S_t proved successful in identifying the model. We will see below that the introduction of the exogenous variables I_t (amount of income) and R_t (amount of rainfall) into the model, with the restrictions that (1) income—while directly affecting the quantity consumers are willing to purchase—does *not* directly affect the amount producers are willing to supply, and (2) rainfall—while directly influencing the quantity producers are willing to supply—does *not* directly affect the amount consumers are willing to buy, were the key factors bringing about identification of the supply and demand equations. Indeed, an assumption that a particular exogenous variable affects some but not all of the endogenous variables in a model is the most commonly used type of restriction in social science research for achieving identification.

Identification and
Underidentification Defined

Ideally, a multiequation model would be one such that, given adequate observation, only one set of parameters would be consistent with both the observations and the model's restrictions. But the problem we faced when looking at the initial wheat market model (equations 10 and 11) was that the information obtainable by observing the two variables in the model—the price of wheat, and the quantity sold—was insufficient to determine the model's parameters. And, in a nutshell, this is the problem with a model that is not identified. In such a case, even with the most complete empirical evidence, our observations would still be consistent with more than one set of parameters. Of course, since a set of

24

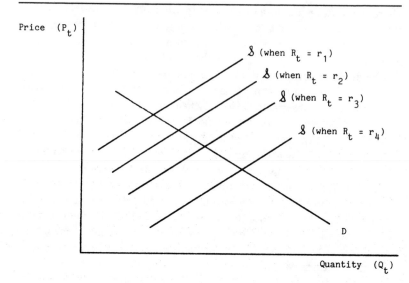

Note: $r_1 < r_2 < r_3 < r_4$

Figure 7: Demand Curve, D, of Equation 10, and Level-Curves for the Supply Surface, $\wp$, of Equation 12

parameters for a model can be thought of as an "explanation" of the process being modeled, our observations would be consistent with multiple explanations. Thus, when faced with a nonidentified model, further observation of empirical relationships among variables will never overcome the problem. To identify a nonidentified model, we must make further a priori assumptions about the variables in the model which are sufficiently restrictive so that only one explanation (i.e., one set of parameters) will be consistent with both the a priori restrictions and the empirical relationships among variables.

Thus far, when discussing the meaning of "identification," we have used statements such as, "An equation is identified if its parameters are uniquely determined by the knowledge derived from 'adequate' or 'complete' observation." To define the concept of identification more precisely, we must clarify what we mean by "adequate" or "complete" observation. We should note first that lack of identification is not a problem of statistical inference; a model will never fail to be identified because of an inadequate sample, or any other problems relating to the task of sampling from a population to estimate parameters. Thus, when defining identification, it is useful to assume that we have complete observation, i.e., complete knowledge of the conditional distribution of the endogenous variables in a model for all values of the exogenous variables. Then we say that an equation in a multiequation model is identified if knowledge of this conditional probability distribution uniquely determines the parameters of the equation.

Christ (1966: Chap. 8) refers to the data that would generate the complete conditional distribution of the endogenous variables of a model given the exogenous variables as a "properly chosen *infinite sample*" (p. 299). By this hypothetical infinite sample he means a sample that contains every possible combination of values of the exogenous variables in the model, and an infinite number of observations for each of the combinations. Using this conception, we can develop an alternative definition of identification. An equation is identified if the acquisition of data for a properly chosen infinite sample would be sufficient to determine a unique set of parameters for the equation; if the equation is identified, only one explanation (i.e., one set of parameters) would be consistent with both the data from the infinite sample and the model's restrictions. Clearly, data for a properly chosen infinite sample cannot be obtained from any finite set of observations; thus, the concept of an infinite sample is strictly hypothetical. But by speaking of such an infinite sample when defining identification, we make it clear that the question of whether an equation is identified is totally independent of any problems of statistical inference occurring because of variation in the data from one finite sample to another.

In contrast, an equation in a model is underidentified or nonidentified if knowledge of the conditional probability distribution of the endogenous variables in the model given the exogenous variables does *not* determine a unique set of parameters for an equation and, instead, multiple sets of parameters for the equation are consistent with the probability distribution. Put differently, an equation is underidentified if data for a properly chosen infinite sample would be consistent with more than one set of parameters for the equation. Clearly, if an *infinite* sample would not give sufficient information to determine an equation's parameters, it is futile to attempt to estimate parameters for the equation using data from a real-world finite sample. Consequently, when an equation in a model is underidentified, meaningful estimates of its parameters cannot be obtained.

Thus, when faced with a nonrecursive model containing an underidentified equation, the model should be modified so that the equation becomes identified before the estimation of parameters is undertaken. To identify a nonidentified equation, a priori assumptions must be made that further restrict the equations in the model. The restrictions may take a variety of forms. Among the possibilities is an assumption that a pair of parameters in the model are equal or have a known ratio. In addition, various types of restrictions on the distributions of error terms in the model are sometimes sufficient for identifying an underidentified equation.[13] In practice, however, the most common type of a priori assumption used to identify equations in a nonrecursive model is a so-called *zero-restriction*, i.e., an assumption that certain parameters in the model are zero, or equivalently that certain variables do not have direct causal effects on certain variables in the model. Of these various types of "identifying restrictions," this book (except in Appendix 2) will be strictly limited in attention to the zero-restriction, as it is the only type that is commonly employed in social science research.

To round out our terminology, we say that a multiequation model is (1) identified (or identifiable) if and only if each of its component equations is identified, and (2) nonidentified if any of its component equations are underidentified. In sum, underidentification is not a problem of measurement or of data availability or quality. Even with the best data—i.e., validly and reliably measured indicators for a large (or even "infinite") sample—a lack of identification will not be overcome. Underidentification, thus, is not a statistical problem; it is a problem of model specification that should be viewed as logically prior to the estimation of parameters through observation from a sample. Identification refers to the hypothetical question, If data for a properly chosen infinite sample were available (which, of course, in the real world will never be), would a unique set of parameters be defined? Indeed, underidentification does not make parameter estimation impossible. Someone can obtain a sample of data and apply a statistical technique—such as OLS regression analysis—to an underidentified equation and obtain parameter estimates. Underidentification simply makes it so that any parameter estimates obtained will be meaningless.

Exact Identification and Overidentification Defined

We have seen that if an equation is underidentified, we must place further restrictions on the model until we achieve a situation in which, if given data from a properly chosen infinite sample, a unique set of parameters for the equation is determined. The resulting equation is then identified. Within the class of identified equations we can distinguish between (1) exactly identified (or just identified) equations, and (2) overidentified equations. An equation in a model is exactly identified if the restrictions placed on the model are minimally sufficient to identify the equation, i.e., if the equation is identified under the restrictions, but underidentified under any proper subset of the restrictions. In contrast, an equation is overidentified if there are additional restrictions on the model beyond a set that is minimally sufficient to identify the equation.[14]

If data for a model from a properly chosen infinite sample were actually available, there would be no need to distinguish between over-identified and exactly identified equations; in either case, the data from the infinite sample would determine a unique set of parameters for the equation. But given that the real world allows us only finite samples for estimating parameters, the distinction between overidentified and exactly identified equations is important. With an exactly identified equation (and data from a finite sample), techniques are available to estimate parameters, and these techniques will generate a unique set of parameter estimates. But when an equation is overidentified, no set of parameter estimates will both (1) be exactly consistent with data from a finite sample, and (2) meet all the a priori restrictions on the model. If we were to drop one or more of the restrictions of a model so that an overidentified equation would become exactly identified, a unique set of parameter estimates, S_1, would be determined. But if we were to drop a different set of restrictions to achieve an equation that is exactly identi-fied, a different unique set of parameter estimates, S_2, would be deter-mined. Thus, relaxing different assumptions of the model generates different estimates for the parameters of an overidentified equation. So, when estimating the parameters of such an equation, we have a statisti-cal problem—the need to resolve the differences between the multiple sets of parameter estimates that are generated when different restric-tions of the model are relaxed, to obtain a single reasonable set of parameter estimates.

Why Some Nonrecursive Models Fail To Be Identified

We have seen that when an equation is underidentified, the informa-tion available from a properly chosen infinite sample is not sufficient to determine a unique set of parameters for the equation. To see more precisely why this information can be insufficient in some nonrecursive models, we will examine several illustrative models—analyzing them from two perspectives: the *reduced-form* perspective, and the *linear combination* perspective. Both these perspectives will shed light on the requirements necessary for an equation in a nonrecursive model to be identified. In addition, these perspectives will suggest a strategy for testing a model for identification that will be incorporated in a proce-dure presented in Chapter 3.

THE REDUCED-FORM PERSPECTIVE

For illustrative purposes, we will begin by examining a *hierarchical nonrecursive* model of voting behavior based on the hypothesized causal effects expressed in Figure 2, and by equations 3 and 4. This model contains the same equations,

$$X_1 = \gamma_{13}Z_3 + \epsilon_1 \tag{14}$$

$$X_2 = \beta_{21}X_1 + \gamma_{23}Z_3 + \epsilon_2 \tag{15}$$

and thus is still hierarchical in nature. But we will relax the assumption that the error terms in the model are uncorrelated with each other in response to the concern that this assumption is unrealistic. Instead, we will make the typical assumptions about error terms in a nonrecursive model introduced in Chapter 1: (1) that the error terms are uncorrelated with all exogenous variables [$\text{cov}(\epsilon_1,Z_3) = \text{cov}(\epsilon_2,Z_3) = 0$], and (2) for convenience, that $E(\epsilon_1) = E(\epsilon_2) = E(X_1) = E(X_2) = E(Z_3) = 0$.

One way to determine whether the equations in a nonrecursive model are identified is to examine the reduced-form equations corresponding to the structural equations for a model. In the structural equation form of a model, each endogenous variable is expressed as a function of the variables (both exogenous and endogenous) that are assumed to have direct causal effects on it, plus an error term, as in equations 14 and 15. However, if the structural equations for a model are reexpressed so that each endogenous variable is written as a function of only exogenous variables in the model and an error term—so that each equation contains only the endogenous variable on the left-hand side—we say that the equations are in reduced form. To place a structural equation in reduced form, we substitute for each endogenous variable on the right-hand side of the equation the expression that defines it in the structural equations. For example, to convert structural equation 15 defining X_2 to reduced form, we substitute $\gamma_{13}Z_3 + \epsilon_1$ for X_1 on the right-hand side of equation 15 and get

$$X_2 = \beta_{21}(\gamma_{13}Z_3 + \epsilon_1) + \gamma_{23}Z_3 + \epsilon_2 \tag{16}$$

Multiplying out all the terms on the right-hand side gives

$$X_2 = \beta_{21}\gamma_{13}Z_3 + \beta_{21}\epsilon_1 + \gamma_{23}Z_3 + \epsilon_2 \tag{17}$$

Finally, rearranging terms produces the following reduced-form equation:

$$X_2 = (\gamma_{23} + \beta_{21}\gamma_{13})Z_3 + (\beta_{21}\epsilon_1 + \epsilon_2) \tag{18}$$

Turning to equation 14, we can see that it is already in reduced form, since no endogenous variables appear in its right-hand side. Thus, together, equations 14 and 18 constitute the reduced-form equations for the model. Finally, if we rename the parameters of these equations such that

$$\pi_{13} = \gamma_{13} \qquad [19.1]$$

$$U = \epsilon_1 \qquad [19.2]$$

$$\pi_{23} = \gamma_{23} + \beta_{21}\gamma_{13} \qquad [19.3]$$

and

$$V = \beta_{21}\epsilon_1 + \epsilon_2 \qquad [19.4]$$

the reduced-form equations for the model can be written

$$X_1 = \pi_{13}Z_3 + U \qquad [20]$$

$$X_2 = \pi_{23}Z_3 + V \qquad [21]$$

where U and V are each uncorrelated with Z_3.[15]

While the reduced-form and structural equations give representations of the same model, there are differences between the two formats. The parameters of the reduced-form equations merely tell us how much each endogenous variable in a model changes in response to a unit change in each of the exogenous variables. In contrast, the structural equations reflect the causal linkages underlying the process being modeled, and thus tell us why the endogenous variables change the amount they do in response to a unit change in an exogenous variable. Furthermore, the reduced-form equations for a model can differ from its structural equation with respect to identification properties. Indeed, it turns out that the reduced-form equations for a nonrecursive model will *always* be identified. The reason for this has to do with the fact that each explanatory variable on the right-hand side of a reduced-form equation will always be uncorrelated with each error term in the model.

To see the implications of this guarantee that the reduced-form equations of a nonrecursive model will be identified, let us return to the model of equations 14 and 15 (with reduced-form equations 20 and 21). Since both reduced-form equations are identified, if data from a properly chosen infinite sample were available, unique values for the parameters π_{13} and π_{23} would be determined. But our ultimate goal is to determine the values of the structural parameters for the model—γ_{13}, γ_{23}, and β_{21}. One strategy toward this end would be to substitute the values of the reduced-form parameters π_{13} and π_{23} in equations 19.1

through 19.4, and then try to solve these equations for the structural parameters. If we are successful—and thus obtain a unique value for each parameter of a particular structural equation—we know the equation is identified. For example, knowledge of the reduced-form parameters π_{13} and π_{23} is sufficient to determine a unique value for the structural parameter γ_{13} of equation 14, as we can solve equations 19.1 through 19.4 to determine that γ_{13} equals π_{13}. Thus, equation 14 is identified. On the other hand, we cannot solve equations 19.1 through 19.4 for unique values for the parameters γ_{23} and β_{21}. Indeed, there are an infinite number of solutions for γ_{23} and β_{21}. This tells us that equation 15 of the model is underidentified.

In general, then, the issue of whether a structural equation in a multiequation model is identified can be reduced to the question, if the reduced-form parameters for the model were exactly known, would there be sufficient information to determine the structural parameters for the equation? A structural equation is exactly identified if and only if its structural parameters are uniquely determined by the reduced-form parameters of the model. An equation is underidentified if knowledge of the reduced-form parameters is insufficient to narrow down a unique solution for the equation's structural parameters. Of course, with non-recursive models with more than two endogenous variables, it is extremely tedious to examine the equations comparable to equalities 19.1 through 19.4 to determine whether the reduced-form parameters uniquely determine the structural parameters for the model. This is why the test for identification presented in Chapter 3 is so useful.

The reduced-form perspective can also be used to determine whether the equations in a nonhierarchical nonrecursive model are identified. To illustrate this, we will examine a modified version of a model developed by Kritzer (1977) concerning the outbreaks of violence at protest events. (This version of the model excludes several of Kritzer's variables; in Chapter 5, though, we will consider Kritzer's complete model.) Our simplified protest violence model is represented by the causal diagram in Figure 8, and by the following equations:

$$X_1 = \beta_{12}X_2 + \gamma_{13}Z_3 + \epsilon_1 \tag{22}$$

$$X_2 = \beta_{21}X_1 + \gamma_{23}Z_3 + \gamma_{24}Z_4 + \epsilon_2 \tag{23}$$

In the model, X_1 represents the level of violence of protestors and X_2 denotes the level of violence of police; these endogenous variables are assumed to be characterized by reciprocal causation. In addition, both are assumed to be directly affected by the exogenous variable Z_3—the nature of civil disobedience committed by protestors. Finally, the extent to which heavy police equipment is available (Z_4) is an exogenous variable thought to have a direct effect on police violence, but only an indirect effect on protestor violence.

To place equation 22 in reduced form, we substitute the expression defining X_2 in equation 23 into equation 22:

$$X_1 = \beta_{12}(\beta_{21}X_1 + \gamma_{23}Z_3 + \gamma_{24}Z_4 + \epsilon_2) + \gamma_{13}Z_3 + \epsilon_1 \qquad [24]$$

If we reexpress the structural equation for X_2 similarly, and rearrange terms in the resulting equation and in equation 24, we derive the following reduced-form equations for the protest violence model of Figure 8:

$$X_1 = \frac{(\gamma_{13} + \beta_{12}\gamma_{23})Z_3 + \beta_{12}\gamma_{24}Z_4 + (\epsilon_1 + \beta_{12}\epsilon_2)}{1 - \beta_{12}\beta_{21}} \qquad [25]$$

$$X_2 = \frac{(\gamma_{23} + \beta_{21}\gamma_{13})Z_3 + \gamma_{24}Z_4 + (\epsilon_2 + \beta_{21}\epsilon_1)}{1 - \beta_{12}\beta_{21}} \qquad [26]$$

Then, these reduced form equations can be written as

$$X_1 = \pi_{13}Z_3 + \pi_{14}Z_4 + U \qquad [27]$$

$$X_2 = \pi_{23}Z_3 + \pi_{24}Z_4 + V, \qquad [28]$$

where

$$\pi_{13} = \frac{\gamma_{13} + \beta_{12}\gamma_{23}}{1 - \beta_{12}\beta_{21}} \qquad [29.1] \qquad \pi_{23} = \frac{\gamma_{23} + \beta_{21}\gamma_{13}}{1 - \beta_{12}\beta_{21}} \qquad [29.4]$$

$$\pi_{14} = \frac{\beta_{12}\gamma_{24}}{1 - \beta_{12}\beta_{21}} \qquad [29.2] \qquad \pi_{24} = \frac{\gamma_{24}}{1 - \beta_{12}\beta_{21}} \qquad [29.5]$$

$$U = \frac{\epsilon_1 + \beta_{12}\epsilon_2}{1 - \beta_{12}\beta_{21}} \qquad [29.3] \qquad V = \frac{\epsilon_2 + \beta_{21}\epsilon_1}{1 - \beta_{12}\beta_{21}} \qquad [29.6]$$

For this model, we can see that knowledge of the reduced-form parameters—π_{13}, π_{14}, π_{23}, and π_{24}—uniquely determines the structural parameters β_{12} and γ_{13} for equation 22, as equalities 29.1 through 29.6 can be solved to give $\beta_{12} = \pi_{14}/\pi_{24}$ and $\gamma_{13} = \pi_{13} - (\pi_{14}\pi_{23}/\pi_{24})$. As such, the structural equation for X_1 in the model of Figure 8 is identified. But we cannot solve equations 29.1 through 29.6 for unique values for the structural parameters—β_{21}, γ_{23}, and γ_{24}—of equation 23; therefore, the equation for X_2 is underidentified.

In the two models we have examined from the reduced-form perspective, all identified equations have been exactly identified. It is useful to examine a final illustrative model that contains an overidentified equation. Here we will consider a model based on research by Duncan, Haller, and Portes (1971) on the influence of adolescents' interaction with peers on their occupational and educational aspirations. We will examine a simplified version of their original model, which excludes variables relating to educational aspiration levels. Later, we will analyze a model closer to Duncan et al.'s original version. Our occupational aspiration model is represented schematically in Figure 9, and formally by the following equations:

$$X_1 = \beta_{12}X_2 + \gamma_{13}Z_3 + \gamma_{14}Z_4 + \epsilon_1 \tag{30}$$

$$X_2 = \beta_{21}X_1 + \gamma_{25}Z_5 + \epsilon_2 \tag{31}$$

The two endogenous variables in the model are X_1 (the level of a male adolescent respondent's occupational aspirations) and X_2 (the level of his friend's occupational aspirations); these variables are assumed to have reciprocal causal effects. For both the respondent and his friend, intelligence (Z_3 for the respondent, Z_5 for the friend) is an exogenous variable assumed to affect aspirations. Also we assume that a measure of the respondent's parental aspirations (i.e., the degree to which he perceives his parents as encouraging him to have a high level of achievement) is available, and that this exogenous variable (Z_4) has a direct effect on the respondent's aspiration level. For this model, substituting parameters and rearranging terms gives the following reduced-form equations:

$$X_1 = \frac{\gamma_{13}Z_3 + \gamma_{14}Z_4 + \beta_{12}\gamma_{25}Z_5 + (\epsilon_1 + \beta_{12}\epsilon_2)}{1 - \beta_{12}\beta_{21}} \tag{32}$$

$$X_2 = \frac{\beta_{21}\gamma_{13}Z_3 + \beta_{21}\gamma_{14}Z_4 + \gamma_{25}Z_5 + (\epsilon_2 + \beta_{21}\epsilon_1)}{1 - \beta_{12}\beta_{21}} \tag{33}$$

These equations can then be rewritten as

$$X_1 = \pi_{13}Z_3 + \pi_{14}Z_4 + \pi_{15}Z_5 + U \tag{34}$$

$$X_2 = \pi_{23}Z_3 + \pi_{24}Z_4 + \pi_{25}Z_5 + V \tag{35}$$

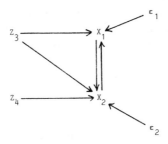

Assumptions: (i) $cov(\epsilon_1, Z_3) = cov(\epsilon_1, Z_4) = cov(\epsilon_2, Z_3)$

$= cov(\epsilon_2, Z_4) = 0$

(ii) $E(X_1) = E(X_2) = E(Z_3) = E(Z_4) = E(\epsilon_1)$

$= E(\epsilon_2) = 0$

Notation: X_1 -- the Level of Violence of Protestors

X_2 -- the Level of Violence of Police

Z_3 -- the Nature of Civil Disobedience Committed by Protestors

Z_4 -- the Extent to Which Heavy Police Equipment is Available

Figure 8: A Causal Diagram of the Nonrecursive Model of Equations 22 and 23

where

$$\pi_{13} = \frac{\gamma_{13}}{1 - \beta_{12}\beta_{21}} \quad [36.1] \qquad \pi_{23} = \frac{\beta_{21}\gamma_{13}}{1 - \beta_{12}\beta_{21}} \quad [36.5]$$

$$\pi_{14} = \frac{\gamma_{14}}{1 - \beta_{12}\beta_{21}} \quad [36.2] \qquad \pi_{24} = \frac{\beta_{21}\gamma_{14}}{1 - \beta_{12}\beta_{21}} \quad [36.6]$$

$$\pi_{15} = \frac{\beta_{12}\gamma_{25}}{1 - \beta_{12}\beta_{21}} \quad [36.3] \qquad \pi_{25} = \frac{\gamma_{25}}{1 - \beta_{12}\beta_{21}} \quad [36.7]$$

$$U = \frac{\epsilon_1 + \beta_{12}\epsilon_2}{1 - \beta_{12}\beta_{21}} \quad [36.4] \qquad V = \frac{\epsilon_2 + \beta_{21}\epsilon_1}{1 - \beta_{12}\beta_{21}} \quad [36.8]$$

Now, if we assume knowledge of the reduced-form parameters and attempt to solve this system of equations for the structural parameters, we find, for example, that $\beta_{21} = \pi_{24}/\pi_{14}$ from equations 36.2 and 36.6, but also that $\beta_{21} = \pi_{23}/\pi_{13}$ from equations 36.1 and 36.5. If structural equations 30 and 31 are an accurate representation of the process being modeled and if data from a "properly chosen infinite sample" were available, having two expressions for determining β_{21} would pose no difficulty, as both expressions would give the same value for β_{21}; thus we would have

$$\beta_{21} = \frac{\pi_{24}}{\pi_{14}} = \frac{\pi_{23}}{\pi_{13}} \qquad [37]$$

However, in practice, the true reduced-form parameters cannot be known, as the infinite sample needed to determine them is unavailable. Instead, we must *estimate* the reduced-form parameters with data from a finite sample—most commonly using OLS regression on equations 34 and 35. But, using a finite sample of cases, there is no guarantee that the reduced-form parameter estimates will satisfy the condition of equality 37. Indeed, our best hope is that this condition will hold only approximately, i.e., that

$$\frac{\hat{\pi}_{24}}{\hat{\pi}_{14}} \simeq \frac{\hat{\pi}_{23}}{\hat{\pi}_{13}}$$

where the symbol $\simeq$ means "approximately equal to," and where the "hats" ($\wedge$) over parameters are used to denote parameter estimates. Thus, in practice there will be no set of estimates of the structural parameters that will satisfy all equalities 36.1 through 36.8 when estimates of the reduced-form parameters are substituted for the true π_{ij}'s in the equations. Instead, for example, the system of equalities 36.1 through 36.8 gives two expressions for $\hat{\beta}_{21}$, namely $\hat{\beta}_{21} = \hat{\pi}_{24}/\hat{\pi}_{14}$ and $\hat{\beta}_{21} = \hat{\pi}_{23}/\hat{\pi}_{13}$. We would hope that the two expressions would yield estimates that are similar in value, but it is inconceivable—given sampling variation—that they will be identical. This leaves us with the statistical problem of resolving the conflicting estimates to determine a single reasonable estimate of the population parameter β_{21}.

A similar situation occurs when any model contains an overidentified equation. The additional restrictions on the model beyond a set "minimally sufficient" to identify the equation make it such that an attempt to solve for the structural parameters given knowledge of the reduced-form parameters will generate multiple expressions for the structural parameters. Then, when estimates of the reduced-form parameters are substituted in the multiple expressions, conflicting estimates for the structural parameters will be generated. When all equations in a model are exactly identified, this situation does not occur, as an attempt to solve for the structural parameters given the reduced-form parameters will always yield unique solutions, and thus a single expression for each of the structural parameters. Then, if estimates of the reduced-form parameters are substituted in these expressions, unique estimates for each of the structural parameters will be determined.

THE LINEAR COMBINATION PERSPECTIVE

A complementary vantage point for assessing whether a multiequation model is identified is the linear combination perspective. A linear combination of a set of equations is an equation that can be obtained by multiplying through each equation in the set by a constant (which can be different for each of the equations) and summing them. For example, $38x + 2y = 82$ is a linear combination of the following equations: (1) $4x + 2y = 8$, (2) $3x + 5y = 17$, and (3) $5x - 6y = 13$. To demonstrate this, we need only note that if we multiply through equation (1) by 7, equation (2) by 0, and equation (3) by 2, we get (1') $28x + 14y = 56$, (2') $0 = 0$, and (3') $10x - 12y = 26$. If we add these three equations, we obtain our objective: $38x + 2y = 82$. By the term "nontrivial" linear combination, I will refer to a linear combination of a set of equations in which none of the constants used in the multiplication is equal to zero.

Armed with these definitions, assume we have a multiequation model presented in structural equation form and satisfying the assumptions of equation system 2. It turns out that linear combinations of the equations in this model have some very important characteristics. First, any model containing equations, each of which is a linear combination of the structural equations in the original model, will necessarily have the same reduced-form equations as the original model. In addition, the converse is true; so we know that the only models that have the same reduced-form equations as our original model are ones containing equations that are linear combinations of the equations in the original model. Second, any equation that is a linear combination of the structural equations in the original model would necessarily be consistent with the data for the original model from a properly chosen infinite sample. The converse is also true; it can be shown that any equation consistent with the data from the infinite sample must be a linear combination of the structural equations for the original model.[16] These characteristics allow us to formulate a condition that must be satisfied for an equation to be identified: An equation in a multiequation model is identified only if all linear combinations of the structural equations in the model (except the equation itself) fail to meet the restrictions placed on the given equation.

To clarify this, we shall reexamine the protest violence model represented schematically in Figure 8, and formally by equations 22 and 23. We start by taking the linear combination of these equations that results from multiplying equation 22 by the nonzero constant λ, and adding the resulting equation to the equation obtained by multiplying equation 23 by the nonzero constant μ. Multiplying by these constants, we get

$$\lambda X_1 = \lambda\beta_{12}X_2 + \lambda\gamma_{13}Z_3 + \lambda\epsilon_1 \qquad [38]$$

$$\mu X_2 = \mu\beta_{21}X_1 + \mu\gamma_{23}Z_3 + \mu\gamma_{24}Z_4 + \mu\epsilon_2. \qquad [39]$$

Adding equations 38 and 39 and collecting terms gives

$$0 = (\lambda\beta_{12} - \mu)X_2 + (\mu\beta_{21} - \lambda)X_1 + (\lambda\gamma_{13} + \mu\lambda_{23})Z_3$$
$$+ (\mu\gamma_{24})Z_4 + (\lambda\epsilon_1 + \mu\epsilon_2) \qquad [40]$$

Next, subtracting $(\lambda\beta_{12} - \mu)X_2$ from both sides of this equation, and then dividing both sides by $-(\lambda\beta_{12} - \mu)$ leaves us with the following linear combination of equations 22 and 23:

$$X_2 = -\frac{\mu\beta_{21} - \lambda}{\lambda\beta_{12} - \mu}(X_1) - \frac{\lambda\gamma_{13} + \mu\gamma_{23}}{\lambda\beta_{12} - \mu}(Z_3)$$

$$-\frac{\mu\gamma_{24}}{\lambda\beta_{12} - \mu}(Z_4) - \frac{\lambda\epsilon_1 + \mu\epsilon_2}{\lambda\beta_{12} - \mu} \qquad [41]$$

This equation, of course, can be written in the following form:

$$X_2 = \beta_{21}^*X_1 + \gamma_{23}^*Z_3 + \gamma_{24}^*Z_4 + \epsilon_2^* \qquad [42]$$

where

$$\beta_{21}^* = -\frac{\mu\beta_{21} - \lambda}{\lambda\beta_{12} - \mu}$$

$$\gamma_{23}^* = -\frac{\lambda\gamma_{13} + \mu\gamma_{23}}{\lambda\beta_{12} - \mu}$$

$$\gamma_{24}^* = -\frac{\mu\gamma_{24}}{\lambda\beta_{12} - \mu}$$

and

$$\epsilon_2^* = -\frac{\lambda\epsilon_1 + \mu\epsilon_2}{\lambda\beta_{12} - \mu}$$

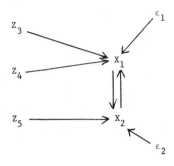

Assumptions: (i) $\text{cov}(\varepsilon_1, Z_3) = \text{cov}(\varepsilon_1, Z_4) = \text{cov}(\varepsilon_1, Z_5) = \text{cov}(\varepsilon_2, Z_3) =$

$\text{cov}(\varepsilon_2, Z_4) = \text{cov}(\varepsilon_2, Z_5) = 0$

(ii) $E(X_1) = E(X_2) = E(Z_3) = E(Z_4) = E(Z_5) = E(\varepsilon_1) =$

$E(\varepsilon_2) = 0$

Notation: X_1 -- Respondent's Occupational Aspiration Level

X_2 -- Friend's Occupational Aspiration Level

Z_3 -- Respondent's Intelligence Level

Z_4 -- Respondent's Parental Aspiration Level

Z_5 -- Friend's Intelligence Level

Figure 9: A Causal Diagram of the Nonrecursive Model of Equations 30 and 31

Finally, it can be shown that error term in equation 42(ε_2*) has mean zero and is uncorrelated with exogenous variables Z_1 and Z_2. Thus, equation 41 is in exactly the same form (i.e., involves the same variables—X_1, X_2, Z_3 and Z_4) as the original structural equation for X_2.

The identical form of equations 23 and 41 ensures that knowledge of the reduced-form parameters for the protest violence model would not determine unique values for the structural parameters of equation 23. Why is this so? We know that the model of equations 22 and 23 has the same reduced-form equations as the model formed by combining equations 22 and 42, since equation 42 is a linear combination of equations 22 and 23. So, if we were given the reduced-form parameters for the protest violence model and we tried to determine the values of the structural parameters for the model, both sets of parameters (1) β_{21}, γ_{23}, and γ_{24}, and (2) β_{21}*, γ_{23}*, and γ_{24}* would prove to be consistent with the reduced-form parameters. Consequently, we know that equation 23 is underidentified. We can also state the logic of this analysis as follows. Assume that data from a properly chosen infinite sample were available for the protest violence model of equations 22 and 23. These data would not permit us to determine unique values for the structural parameters of equation 23, because while β_{21}, γ_{23}, and γ_{24}, are consistent with the data, so too are the parameters $\beta*_{21}$, $\gamma*_{23}$, and $\gamma*_{24}$. So too are the parameters for any of the infinite number of nontrivial linear combination of equations 22 and 23. Thus, we see again that equation 23 is underidentified. In essence, we have seen that it is possible to form a linear combination of the equations of the protest violence model which meets all the restrictions placed on equation 23 (i.e., contains exactly the same variables as equation 23). This is sufficient to verify that equation 23 is not identified.

What about structural equation 22 in the model? In contrast to our earlier situation, if (as is assumed) γ_{24} does not equal zero, *any* nontrivial linear combination of equations 22 and 23 will necessarily contain a term with a nonzero parameter (e.g., $\mu\gamma_{24}$) for Z_4. Thus, while all nontrivial linear combinations of equations 22 and 23 will be consistent with a properly chosen infinite sample for the model, none of these linear combinations will meet the restriction on equation 22 that the coefficient for Z_2 is zero. Thus, data from a properly chosen infinite sample are sufficient to determine uniquely the structural parameters of equation 22; this confirms that equation 22 is identified.

In general, then, one test for the identification of a structural equation in a multiequation model consists of an analysis of the possibility of obtaining a different equation of the same form (i.e., including exactly the same variables) as the equation in question by taking a linear combination of some or all of the structural equations in the model. If it can be shown that this is not possible for a certain equation, we can be sure the equation is identified. Conversely, if we can find a linear combination of some or all the equations in the model (apart from the equation in question itself) which includes exactly the same variables as the equation in question, we can be sure that the equation is underidentified. This suggests an expectation that the more variables in a model assumed to have zero-parameters in a given equation (i.e., the more variables "left out" of the equation), the greater is the likelihood the equation will be identified, as the zero-restrictions make it more difficult to form a linear combination of the equations in the model that is indistinguishable in form from the given equation. This is a key rule we will keep in mind when we turn, in Chapter 4, to the art of modifying nonidentified nonrecursive models to achieve identification.

3. TESTING FOR IDENTIFICATION

We have seen that we can test whether a nonrecursive model is identified using either the reduced-form or linear combination perspectives. These two perspectives are mathematically equivalent in the sense that they lead to the same conclusion about whether or not the equations in a model are identified. They also give us conditions that are both *necessary* and *sufficient* for identification; i.e., each perspective generates a condition that guarantees that an equation is underidentified, as well as a condition that ensures that an equation is identified. However, in a practical sense, both perspectives are extremely tedious and time consuming to apply to any but the most simple of nonrecursive models. Fortunately, two more practical tests for identification are available. One is the *rank condition*, which also is both necessary and sufficient for identification. In this chapter I will present an algorithm that is adapted from and mathematically equivalent to the rank condition. The other common test for identification is the *order condition*, which has the advantage of extreme ease of application but the disadvantage that, while it serves as a necessary condition for identification, it is not sufficient.

The Order Condition

Assume that we have a nonrecursive model expressed by a system of structural equations. We let

m = the number of endogenous variables in the model, and

k = the number of exogenous variables in the model.

We continue to assume that all variables and error terms have a mean of zero.[17] We also continue to restrict our attention to nonrecursive models in which the only other assumption made about error terms is that each error term is uncorrelated with all exogenous variables in the model. Once again, I warn the reader that, for a particular substantive model, if this assumption is not reasonable, or if the reader is prepared to make an even stronger set of assumptions about error terms, the tests for identification presented in this chapter are not applicable without modification. (See Appendix 2.)

The most commonly used method of testing for identification is a simple counting technique called the order condition. With this technique, each equation in a model is tested for identification separately. Assume we have a structural equation we want to test. For the equation to be identified, it is necessary that the number of exogenous variables excluded from the equation be greater than or equal to the number of endogenous variables included in the equation as explanatory variables. Thus, if we let

k_e = the number of exogenous variables in the model excluded from the structural equation being tested, and

m_i = the number of endogenous variables in the model included in the equation being tested (including the one being explained on the left-hand side),

the order condition states that for the equation to be identified, it must satisfy the requirement that

$$k_e \geqslant m_i - 1 \qquad [43]$$

(1 is subtracted from the right-hand side because m_i takes into account both the explanatory endogenous variables and the endogenous variable being explained.)

Some simple arithmetic will produce an alternative and equivalent way of formulating the order condition. If we let

m_e = the number of endogenous variables in the model excluded from the structural equation being tested,

we can add m_e to both sides of condition 43 to get

$$m_e + k_e \geqslant m_e + m_i - 1 \qquad [44]$$

But $m_e + m_i = m$ (the total number of endogenous variables in the model); so condition 44 is equivalent to

$$m_e + k_e \geqslant m - 1 \qquad [45]$$

Thus, for an equation to be identified, it is necessary that the number of variables (either exogenous or endogenous) excluded from the equation must equal or exceed the number of structural equations in the model minus one.

These two versions of the order condition are useful tools for speedy diagnosis of some equations that are underidentified; if an equation fails to satisfy the order condition, the equation must be underidentified. But the limitation of the order condition must also be recognized; the order condition—while necessary for identification—is not sufficient. Thus, the success of an equation in satisfying the order condition should not be relied on for evidence that the equation is identified. Before assuming that an equation is identified—and, thus, that parameter estimation can reasonably be undertaken—the equation should be tested using the rank condition.

The Rank Condition

The rank condition is a necessary and sufficient condition for identification, which is adapted from the procedure of testing an equation for identification using the linear combination perspective. Typically, the condition is presented in a format that requires a knowledge of matrix algebra. However, this chapter presents an algorithm that is mathematically equivalent to the rank condition, but which can be used by someone with no previous exposure to matrix algebra.[18]

The basic approach of the algorithm is to represent the coefficients of the variables in a model in a rectangular table or matrix with a row corresponding to each structural equation in the model. For example, if we rewrite structural equations 22 and 23 (corresponding to the model in Figure 8) as

$$0 = -X_1 + \beta_{12}X_2 + \gamma_{13}Z_3 + \epsilon_1 \qquad [46]$$

$$0 = \beta_{21}X_1 - X_2 + \gamma_{23}Z_3 + \gamma_{24}Z_4 + \epsilon_2 \qquad [47]$$

we could represent these structural equations by the matrix

$$
\begin{array}{cccc}
 & X_1 & X_2 & Z_3 & Z_4 \\
X_1 & \begin{bmatrix} -1 & \beta_{12} & \gamma_{13} & 0 \\ \beta_{21} & -1 & \gamma_{23} & \gamma_{24} \end{bmatrix} \\
X_2
\end{array}
$$

It can be shown that we can preserve all the information we need to test for identificaton by reducing each of the coefficients in the matrix to a zero (0) or an asterisk (*), depending on whether a given variable is or is not included in an equation. Then we can manipulate the 0's and *'s to simulate how the coefficients in the corresponding equations would be changed if we multiplied one equation by a constant and added the resulting equation to another (i.e., if we took linear combinations of the equations).

THE ALGORITHM

We continue to assume that we have a nonrecursive model expressed by a set of structural equations, in which each error term is assumed uncorrelated with all exogenous variables, and all variables and error terms are assumed to have a mean of zero. Also, m, k, m_i, m_e, and k_e are as defined in the section above. We form a so-called *system matrix* with m rows and $m+k$ columns as follows. On the left-side margin of the system matrix, list the endogenous variables in the model in any order. On the top margin of the system matrix, list all the variables in the model (both endogenous and exogenous) in any order.

Each row of the system matrix corresponds to the structural equation defining the endogenous variable in the left margin of that row. Considering one structural equation at a time to determine the entries in the matrix row corresponding to it, place an asterisk in each column corresponding to each variable included on either the right- or left-hand side of the structural equation. Place zero in all other matrix positions of that row.[19] Now do the same for all other structural equations in the model, i.e., for all other rows of the system matrix. The result is a matrix containing a zero or an asterisk in every position. This system matrix contains all the information required to test whether or not any equation in the model is identified.

As with the order condition, each equation must be tested separately for identification using the algorithm. Also, it is useful to build the order condition into the algorithm as a first step. So for a particular equation in the model to be identified, it is necessary that k_e be greater than or equal to m_i minus one. Thus, if $k_e < m_i - 1$, the equation is necessarily underidentified and the remaining procedures of the algorithm for the equation being considered are not needed. But, if $k_e \geq m_i - 1$ for the equation, the following steps must be performed.

Call the row of the system matrix corresponding to the equation being tested for identification the *test row*. The first step is to draw a line through the test row.[20] Also draw a line through any column containing an asterisk in the test row. Now, rewrite the system matrix deleting (1) the row that is crossed out (i.e., the test row) and (2) all the columns that are crossed out. The remaining submatrix is called the *collapsed matrix* for the given test row.

We must make three final definitions: (1) Two rows of a matrix are said to be *identical* if, in each column of the matrix, the two rows contain the same entry. (2) The *leading asterisk-entry* of a row is defined as the first asterisk in the row as one scans across the row beginning in the left-most column of the matrix. (3) We say that a matrix is in *simple form* if each column that contains the leading asterisk-entry of some row has all other entries equal to zero.[21] To illustrate these definitions, consider the following 3×3 matrix:

$$
Row \quad
\begin{array}{c}
 \\
1 \\
2 \\
3
\end{array}
\begin{array}{ccc}
\multicolumn{3}{c}{Column} \\
1 & 2 & 3 \\
\left[\begin{array}{ccc}
* & 0 & * \\
* & * & 0 \\
* & 0 & *
\end{array}\right]
\end{array}
$$

First, we see that rows 1 and 3 of this matrix are identical, as both these rows have a zero in column 2 and asterisks in all other columns. Second, this matrix is not in simple form. To show this we need only note, for instance, that column 1 contains the leading asterisk entry of row 1, and also contains an additional asterisk in row 2. The rationale behind the definition of simple form will become clear as the procedure is developed. In essence, the strategy will be to manipulate the collapsed matrix according to rules laid out below in order to put the matrix into simple form. Once in simple form, a quick glance at the matrix will tell whether or not the equation corresponding to the test row is identified.

The procedure for analyzing a collapsed matrix is outlined in flow-chart form in Figure 10. The steps in the flowchart complete the identification algorithm. I now offer several examples of how the entire procedure can be used to test the equations of a model for identification.

An occupational and educational aspiration model. We will now expand the occupational aspiration model presented above to a model closer in form to the one developed by Duncan et al. (1971). This model—presented schematically in Figure 11—contains four endogenous variables: (1) the level of a male adolescent respondent's occupational aspirations, X_1; (2) the level of his friend's occupational aspira-

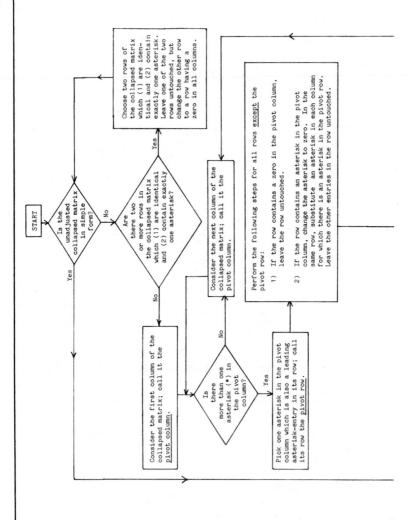

START

Is the unadjusted collapsed matrix in simple form?

Yes

No

Are there two or more rows in the collapsed matrix which (1) are identical and (2) contain exactly one asterisk?

Yes

Choose two rows of the collapsed matrix which (1) are identical and (2) contain exactly one asterisk. Leave one of the two rows untouched, but change the other row to a row having a zero in all columns.

No

Consider the first column of the collapsed matrix; call it the pivot column.

Is there more than one asterisk (*) in the pivot column?

No

Consider the next column of the collapsed matrix; call it the pivot column.

Yes

Pick one asterisk in the pivot column which is also a leading asterisk-entry in its row; call its row the pivot row.

Perform the following steps for all rows except the pivot row:

1) If the row contains a zero in the pivot column, leave the row untouched.

2) If the row contains an asterisk in the pivot column, change the asterisk to zero. In the same row, substitute an asterisk in each column for which there is an asterisk in the pivot row. Leave the other entries in the row untouched.

44

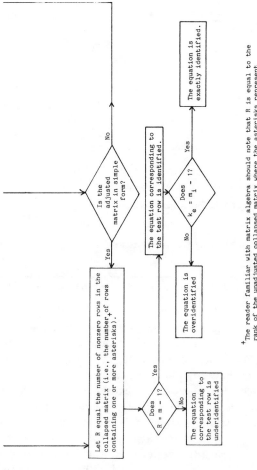

The flowchart contains the following elements:

Let R equal the number of nonzero rows in the collapsed matrix (i.e., the number of rows containing one or more asterisks).[+]

Is the adjusted matrix in simple form?

Yes → Does R = m - 1?

Yes → The equation corresponding to the test row is identified.

No → The equation corresponding to the test row is underidentified

Does $k_e = m_i - 1$?

No → The equation is overidentified

Yes → The equation is exactly identified.

[+] The reader familiar with matrix algebra should note that R is equal to the rank of the unadjusted collapsed matrix where the asterisks represent structural parameters not assumed to be zero.

Figure 10: Procedure for Analyzing a Collapsed Matrix

45

46

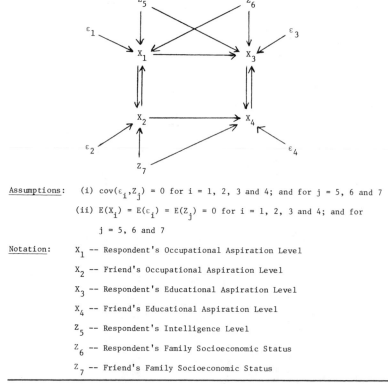

Assumptions: (i) $\text{cov}(\varepsilon_i, Z_j) = 0$ for $i = 1, 2, 3$ and 4; and for $j = 5, 6$ and 7

(ii) $E(X_i) = E(\varepsilon_i) = E(Z_j) = 0$ for $i = 1, 2, 3$ and 4; and for $j = 5, 6$ and 7

Notation: X_1 -- Respondent's Occupational Aspiration Level

X_2 -- Friend's Occupational Aspiration Level

X_3 -- Respondent's Educational Aspiration Level

X_4 -- Friend's Educational Aspiration Level

Z_5 -- Respondent's Intelligence Level

Z_6 -- Respondent's Family Socioeconomic Status

Z_7 -- Friend's Family Socioeconomic Status

Figure 11: A Causal Diagram of the Nonrecursive Model of Equations 48 through 51

tions, X_2; (3) the level of the respondent's educational aspirations, X_3; and (4) the level of his friend's educational aspirations, X_4. We assume that the two occupational aspiration variables are characterized by reciprocal causation, and that the same is the case for the two educational aspiration variables. Furthermore, we expect that for both the respondent and his friend, occupational aspirations are a direct cause of educational aspirations. Also, we assume that an indicator of intelligence is available (but only for the respondent) and we specify that the respondent's intelligence (Z_5) has direct effects on both his occupational and educational aspirations.[22] Finally, we introduce both the respondent's and his friend's family socioeconomic status into the model as exogenous variables (Z_6 and Z_7), affecting both occupational and educational aspirations. Therefore, the structural equations for the model are as follows:

$$X_1 = \beta_{12}X_2 + \gamma_{15}Z_5 + \gamma_{16}Z_6 + \epsilon_1 \qquad [48]$$

$$X_2 = \beta_{21}X_1 + \gamma_{27}Z_7 + \epsilon_2 \qquad [49]$$

$$X_3 = \beta_{31}X_1 + \beta_{34}X_4 + \gamma_{35}Z_5 + \gamma_{36}Z_6 + \epsilon_3 \qquad [50]$$

$$X_4 = \beta_{42}X_2 + \beta_{43}X_3 + \gamma_{47}Z_7 + \epsilon_4, \qquad [51]$$

where each of the error terms (ϵ_1, ϵ_2, ϵ_3, and ϵ_4) is assumed to be uncorrelated with each of the exogenous variables (Z_5, Z_6, and Z_7), and all variables and error terms are assumed to have a mean of zero.

For this system of structural equations, m = 4 and k = 3, and the system matrix for the model can be formed as follows:

	X_1	X_2	X_3	X_4	Z_5	Z_6	Z_7
X_1	*	*	0	0	*	*	0
X_2	*	*	0	0	0	0	*
X_3	*	0	*	*	*	*	0
X_4	0	*	*	*	0	0	*

First, let us test for identification structural equation 48 defining X_1. For this equation, $k_e \geq m_i - 1$, as $k_e = 1$ and $m_i = 2$. Thus, the order condition is satisfied, and we must proceed with the algorithm. Drawing lines through the test row (the X_1 row) and the X_1, X_2, Z_5, and Z_6 columns (those containing an asterisk in the test row), we get:

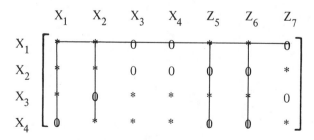

48

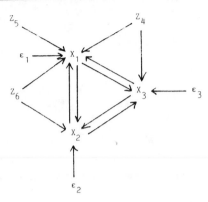

Assumptions: (i) $\text{cov}(\epsilon_i, Z_j) = 0$ for $i = 1$, 2 and 3; and for $j = 4$, 5 and 6

(ii) $E(X_i) = E(\epsilon_i) = E(Z_j) = 0$ for $i = 1$, 2 and 3; and for

$j = 4$, 5 and 6

Notation: X_1 -- Political Party ID

X_2 -- Comparative Candidate Evaluation

X_3 -- Policy/Issue Positions

Z_4 -- Education

Z_5 -- Father's Political Party ID

Z_6 -- Partisan Voting History

Figure 12: A Causal Diagram of the Nonrecursive Model of Equations 52, 53, and 54

Hence, the collapsed matrix for the test row is:

$$
\begin{array}{cc}
 & \textit{Column} \\
 & \begin{array}{ccc} 1 & 2 & 3 \end{array} \\
\textit{Row} \begin{array}{c} 1 \\ 2 \\ 3 \end{array} &
\begin{bmatrix}
0 & 0 & * \\
* & * & 0 \\
* & * & *
\end{bmatrix}
\end{array}
$$

We now adjust the collapsed matrix using the procedure on the flowchart in Figure 10. First, we note that the unadjusted collapsed matrix is not in simple form (e.g., row 2 has its leading asterisk-entry in column 1, but column 1 contains two asterisks). Then we note that no two rows in the collapsed matrix are identical. So we start with column 1 as the *pivot column* (see Figure 10 for a definition). Since there is more than one asterisk in the pivot column (i.e., asterisks in rows 2 and 3), we must choose either row 2 or row 3 as the *pivot row* (defined in Figure 10). Note that the choice will not affect the value of R (defined in Figure 10) for the collapsed matrix, although it will affect the position of zeros and asterisks in the resulting simple-form matrix.

Let us make row 2 the pivot row. We must examine all other rows in the matrix (i.e., rows 1 and 3) separately. Since row 1 contains a zero in the pivot column (column 1), we leave row 1 untouched. But row 3 contains an asterisk in the pivot column and, thus, must be adjusted. In accordance with the flowchart's instructions, we change the asterisk in row 3/column 1 to a zero. Then, since the pivot row contains an asterisk in column 2, we must substitute an asterisk for the entry in row 3/column 2. (Of course, in this example, this entry was already an asterisk prior to the substitution, so the substitution really results in no change.) After these adjustments, the matrix becomes

$$
\begin{array}{c}
\quad\quad\quad Column \\
\quad\quad\quad
\begin{array}{ccc}
1 & 2 & 3
\end{array} \\
\begin{array}{c}
\\ Row \\ \\
\end{array}
\begin{array}{c}
1 \\ 2 \\ 3
\end{array}
\left[
\begin{array}{ccc}
0 & 0 & * \\
* & * & 0 \\
0 & * & *
\end{array}
\right]
\end{array}
$$

The matrix is not yet in simple form (e.g., row 3 has its leading asterisk-entry in column 2, but column 2 contains two asterisks). So we go back in the flowchart and make column 2 the pivot column. Column 2 contains more than one asterisk, but only one leading asterisk-entry (in row 3). Thus, row 3 must be made the pivot row. Since row 1 contains a zero in the pivot column, we leave row 1 untouched. But row 2 contains an asterisk in the pivot column, and must be adjusted. We convert the asterisk in row 2/column 2 to a zero, and substitute an asterisk in row 2/column 3. These adjustments produce the following matrix:

$$
\begin{array}{c}
\quad\quad\quad Column \\
\quad\quad\quad
\begin{array}{ccc}
1 & 2 & 3
\end{array} \\
\begin{array}{c}
\\ Row \\ \\
\end{array}
\begin{array}{c}
1 \\ 2 \\ 3
\end{array}
\left[
\begin{array}{ccc}
0 & 0 & * \\
* & 0 & * \\
0 & * & *
\end{array}
\right]
\end{array}
$$

This matrix is still not in simple form, as column 3 contains both the leading asterisk-entry of row 1 and two other asterisks. So we go back in the flowchart and make column 3 the pivot column. Of the three asterisks in column 3, only the one in row 1 is a leading asterisk-entry. Thus, row 1 must be the pivot row. Then we must adjust rows 2 and 3, since both these rows contain an asterisk in the pivot column; we change all other asterisks in column 3 (i.e., those in row 2/column 3 and in row 3/column 3) to zeros, and are left with

$$
\begin{array}{cc}
 & Column \\
 & \begin{array}{ccc} 1 & 2 & 3 \end{array} \\
Row \begin{array}{c} 1 \\ 2 \\ 3 \end{array} &
\begin{bmatrix}
0 & 0 & * \\
* & 0 & 0 \\
0 & * & 0
\end{bmatrix}
\end{array}
$$

This matrix is in simple form since there is only one asterisk in each of columns 1, 2, and 3. Therefore, no further adjustments of the matrix are required.

Since there are no rows in the simple-form matrix without one or more asterisks, $R = 3$, and since we already have determined that $m = 4$, $r = m - 1$. Thus, structural equation 48 for X_1 is identified. Finally, since $k_e = (m_i - 1) = 1$, we know that the equation is exactly identified.

Let us move to equation 49 in the aspiration model and test it for identification. For this equation, the order condition is satisfied, as $k_e = 2$, $m_i = 2$; therefore $k_e > m_i - 1$. We draw lines through the test row (the X_2 row) and through the X_1, X_2, and Z_7 columns, and upon deleting the entries from these rows and columns, we are left with the following collapsed matrix for the test row:

$$
\begin{array}{cc}
 & Column \\
 & \begin{array}{cccc} 1 & 2 & 3 & 4 \end{array} \\
Row \begin{array}{c} 1 \\ 2 \\ 3 \end{array} &
\begin{bmatrix}
0 & 0 & * & * \\
* & * & * & * \\
* & * & 0 & 0
\end{bmatrix}
\end{array}
$$

This collapsed matrix is not in simple form; also, no two rows in the collapsed matrix are identical. We make column 1 the pivot column, and choose row 3 as the pivot row. Row 1 contains a zero in the pivot column, so we leave row 1 untouched. Row 2, however, contains an asterisk in the pivot column and thus must be adjusted. The resulting adjusted matrix is as follows:

$$
\begin{array}{c}
 & & \textit{Column} & \\
 & & 1 \quad 2 \quad 3 \quad 4 & \\
 & 1 & \begin{bmatrix} 0 & 0 & * & * \\ 0 & * & * & * \\ * & * & 0 & 0 \end{bmatrix} \\
\textit{Row} & 2 & \\
 & 3 &
\end{array}
$$

Then column 2 becomes the pivot column, which necessitates that row 2 be the pivot row. Row 1 is left alone, but row 3 is adjusted to produce the following matrix, which still is not yet in simple form:

$$
\begin{array}{c}
 & & \textit{Column} & \\
 & & 1 \quad 2 \quad 3 \quad 4 & \\
 & 1 & \begin{bmatrix} 0 & 0 & * & * \\ 0 & * & * & * \\ * & 0 & * & * \end{bmatrix} \\
\textit{Row} & 2 & \\
 & 3 &
\end{array}
$$

Next, we make column 3 the pivot column, and row 1 the pivot row. Following the necessary adjustments to rows 2 and 3, we achieve the following matrix:

$$
\begin{array}{c}
 & & \textit{Column} & \\
 & & 1 \quad 2 \quad 3 \quad 4 & \\
 & 1 & \begin{bmatrix} 0 & 0 & * & * \\ 0 & * & 0 & * \\ * & 0 & 0 & * \end{bmatrix} \\
\textit{Row} & 2 & \\
 & 3 &
\end{array}
$$

This matrix is in simple form; thus, no further adjustments are needed. Again, we find $R = 3$, and since $m = 4$, $R = m - 1$. Thus, structural equation 49 defining X_2 is identified. Finally, recalling the test of the order condition for the equation, we know that $k_e > m_i - 1$; therefore, equation 49 is overidentified.

Turning to structural equation 50, here, $k_e = 1$ and $m_i = 3$. So equation 50 does not satisfy the order condition and, thus, is necessarily under-identified. Finally, applying the algorithm to equation 51 would show that it is exactly identified, as we would ultimately find that $R = 3 = m - 1$, and that $k_e = 2 = m_i - 1$. Thus, the identification properties of the aspiration model of Figure 11 can be stated in full: Structural equations 48, 49, and 51 are identified—with the equations for X_1 and X_4 exactly identified, and the equation for X_2 overidentified—but equation 50 (defining X_3) is underidentified. Thus, given adequate data, we can reasonably estimate the parameters of equations 48, 49, and 51, but not those of equation 50. Thus, we will have to (in Chapter 4) modify the aspiration model to identify all of its structural equations.

A model of voting behavior. For illustrative purposes, we will also test an expanded version of the voting behavior model of Figure 4 for identification. We add to this model two exogenous variables drawn from Page and Jones's (1979) research: (1) father's party identification, Z_5, which is assumed to have a direct effect on the individual's party ID, and (2) the individual's "partisan voting history," Z_6, which is assumed to be a direct cause of both party ID and comparative candidate evaluations. With these additions, we have the model depicted in Figure 12 and represented by the following equations:

$$X_1 = \beta_{12}X_2 + \beta_{13}X_3 + \gamma_{14}Z_4 + \gamma_{15}Z_5 + \gamma_{16}Z_6 + \epsilon_1 \qquad [52]$$

$$X_2 = \beta_{21}X_1 + \beta_{23}X_3 + \gamma_{26}Z_6 + \epsilon_2 \qquad [53]$$

$$X_3 = \beta_{31}X_1 + \beta_{32}X_2 + \gamma_{34}Z_4 + \epsilon_3 \qquad [54]$$

For this model, $m = k = 3$, and a system matrix can be formed as follows:

	X_1	X_2	X_3	Z_4	Z_5	Z_6
X_1	*	*	*	*	*	*
X_2	*	*	*	0	0	*
X_3	*	*	*	*	0	0

We can easily see that structural equation 52 for X_1 in the voting behavior model is underidentified by the order condition, as $k_e = 0$ and $m_i = 3$, and thus $k_e < m_i - 1$. But equation 53 satisfies the order condition

($k_e = 2$; $m_i = 3$). Thus, we form a collapsed matrix for the equation by deleting from the system matrix the X_2 row and the X_1, X_2, X_3, and Z_6 columns:

$$
\begin{array}{c}
\textit{Column} \\
\begin{array}{cc}
1 & 2
\end{array} \\
\textit{Row} \quad
\begin{array}{c}
1 \\
2
\end{array}
\begin{bmatrix}
* & * \\
* & 0
\end{bmatrix}
\end{array}
$$

We make column 1 the pivot column and choose row 2 as the pivot row. Adjusting row 1 according to the rules leaves us with a matrix in simple form:

$$
\begin{array}{c}
\textit{Column} \\
\begin{array}{cc}
1 & 2
\end{array} \\
\textit{Row} \quad
\begin{array}{c}
1 \\
2
\end{array}
\begin{bmatrix}
0 & * \\
* & 0
\end{bmatrix}
\end{array}
$$

Therefore, R equals 2, which also equals $m - 1$, and the equation is identified; furthermore, since $k_e = m_i - 1$, equation 53 is exactly identified.

The algorithm also shows that structural equation 54 is exactly identified. The collapsed matrix for this equation is

$$
\begin{array}{c}
\textit{Column} \\
\begin{array}{cc}
1 & 2
\end{array} \\
\textit{Row} \quad
\begin{array}{c}
1 \\
2
\end{array}
\begin{bmatrix}
* & * \\
0 & *
\end{bmatrix}
\end{array}
$$

Adjusting this matrix would demonstrate that $R = 2 = m - 1$ and that, as with the previous equation, $k_e = 2 = m_i - 1$. Consequently, two of the equations of the voting behavior model are exactly identified, while the third is underidentified; so modification of the model is required. Before addressing the topic of how to modify nonidentified models to achieve identification, we return to the aspiration example.

The Insufficiency of the Order Condition:
An Illustration

In the two previous applications of the algorithm, each equation that satisfied the order condition turned out to be identified. To thwart the temptation to note this pattern and begin using the order condition as a condition sufficient (as well as necessary) for identification, we will consider an expanded version of the educational and occupational aspiration model. This revised model is presented in Figure 13 and represented by the following structural equations:[23]

$$X_1 = \beta_{12}X_2 + \beta_{19}X_9 + \gamma_{15}Z_5 + \gamma_{16}Z_6 + \epsilon_1 \tag{55}$$

$$X_2 = \beta_{21}X_1 + \beta_{2,10}X_{10} + \gamma_{27}Z_7 + \gamma_{28}Z_8 + \epsilon_2 \tag{56}$$

$$X_3 = \beta_{31}X_1 + \beta_{34}X_4 + \beta_{39}X_9 + \gamma_{35}Z_5 + \gamma_{36}Z_6 + \epsilon_3 \tag{57}$$

$$X_4 = \beta_{42}X_2 + \beta_{43}X_3 + \beta_{4,10}X_{10} + \gamma_{47}Z_7 + \gamma_{48}Z_8 + \epsilon_4 \tag{58}$$

$$X_9 = \gamma_{95}Z_5 + \gamma_{96}Z_6 + \epsilon_9 \tag{59}$$

$$X_{10} = \gamma_{10,7}Z_7 + \gamma_{10,8}Z_8 + \epsilon_{10} \tag{60}$$

This model differs from that of Figure 11 in that we now assume that an indicator of friend's intelligence (Z_8) is available. We also add to the model two endogenous variables: Respondent's Parental Aspiration Level (X_9), and Friend's Parental Aspiration Level (X_{10}). An adolescent's parental aspirations are assumed to affect his educational and occupational aspirations, and to be affected by his intelligence and family socioeconomic status.

The new aspiration model is, therefore, one for which m = 6 and k = 4, and we can form a system matrix for the model as follows:

	X_1	X_2	X_3	X_4	X_9	X_{10}	Z_5	Z_6	Z_7	Z_8
X_1	*	*	0	0	*	0	*	*	0	0
X_2	*	*	0	0	0	*	0	0	*	*
X_3	*	0	*	*	*	0	*	*	0	0
X_4	0	*	*	*	0	*	0	0	*	*
X_9	0	0	0	0	*	0	*	*	0	0
X_{10}	0	0	0	0	0	*	0	0	*	*

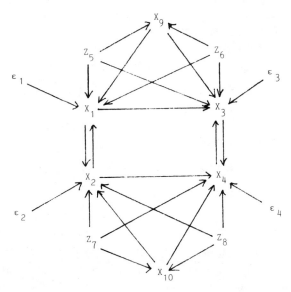

Assumptions: (i) $cov(\varepsilon_i, Z_j) = 0$ for $i = 1, 2, 3, 4, 9$ and 10; and for

$j = 5, 6, 7$ and 8

(ii) $E(X_i) = E(\varepsilon_i) = E(Z_j) = 0$ for $i = 1, 2, 3, 4, 9$ and

10; and for $j = 5, 6, 7$ and 8

Notation: X_1 -- Respondent's Occupational Aspiration Level

X_2 -- Friend's Occupational Aspiration Level

X_3 -- Respondent's Educational Aspiration Level

X_4 -- Friend's Educational Aspiration Level

Z_5 -- Respondent's Intelligence Level

Z_6 -- Respondent's Family Socioeconomic Status

Z_7 -- Friend's Family Socioeconomic Status

Z_8 -- Friend's Intelligence Level

X_9 -- Respondent's Parental Aspiration Level

X_{10} -- Friend's Parental Aspiration Level

Figure 13: A Causal Diagram of the Nonrecursive Model of Equations 55 through 60

Consider structural equation 55 in the model. For this equation, $k_e = 2$ and $m_i = 3$. Therefore, $k_e = m_i - 1$ and the order condition is satisfied. If we continue with the algorithm for this equation, we will derive the following collapsed matrix:

$$
\begin{array}{c}
 & & \multicolumn{5}{c}{Column} \\
 & & 1 & 2 & 3 & 4 & 5 \\
 & 1 & 0 & 0 & * & * & * \\
 & 2 & * & * & 0 & 0 & 0 \\
Row & 3 & * & * & * & * & * \\
 & 4 & 0 & 0 & 0 & 0 & 0 \\
 & 5 & 0 & 0 & * & * & *
\end{array}
$$

Performing the adjustments to get this matrix in simple form would eventually demonstrate that $R = 4$. (It is immediately clear that R must be less than 5, because row 4 of the matrix will never be adjusted in any of the steps of the algorithm.) But since $m = 6$, $R \neq m - 1$; thus, the equation is underidentified. Note that the equation fails to be identified, *even though the order condition is satisfied.* Indeed, an examination of equation 55 from the linear combination perspective demonstrates why the equation is underidentified. The problem is that equation 59, in the same model, contains some of the variables of equation 55 (i.e., X_9, Z_5, and Z_6) but no variables that are not also included in equation 55. Thus, any nontrivial linear combination of equations 55 and 59 will contain exactly the same variables as equation 55; consequently, by the linear combination perspective, equation 55 is underidentified.

In conclusion, the general point to remember is that the order condition is not sufficient; while it is a useful tool to verify that some equations are underidentified, it should not be relied upon to demonstrate that an equation is identified. If an equation satisfies the order condition, the full algorithm must be applied to test whether or not the equation satisfies the rank condition as well.

4. MODIFYING NONIDENTIFIED MODELS

There are several techniques available for estimating the parameters of equations in identified nonrecursive models. But, for underidentified equations, no estimation technique is available that can overcome the lack of identification and generate meaningful parameter estimates. Does this mean that when faced with a nonidentified model, the only course available is to shrug one's shoulders, and switch to a different substantive area of research? The answer, of course, is no. A nonidentified model can be "identified" by imposing additional restrictions on the equations in the model. Several of these types of restrictions were reviewed in Chapter 2, but by far the most common in social science research are *zero-restrictions*: assumptions that certain variables can be omitted from certain structural equations in the model or, equivalently, that certain parameters of the model are equal to zero.

Indeed, the examination of the identification problem from the linear combination perspective in Chapter 2 suggested that the more variables in the model that are left out of a particular equation (i.e., the more variables that are restricted to having parameters equal to zero in the equation), the more likely the equation is to be identified. And the identification characteristics of the illustrative models tested in the previous chapter are consistent with this rule of thumb. For example, in the voting behavior model of Figure 12, the only nonidentified structural equation is equation 52 for X_1. Also, of all the equations of the model, this equation has the fewest zero restrictions. Equations 53 and 54 each have two parameters assumed equal to zero (those for Z_4 and Z_5 in equation 53, and for Z_5 and Z_6 in equation 54). In contrast, equation 52 has no zero restrictions, as all the variables included in the model also appear in structural equation 52. Similarly, in the aspiration model of Figure 11, the only structural equation that is underidentified is equation 50 which defines X_3, and of the four structural equations in the model, equation 50 has the fewest deleted variables. In any event, the rule of thumb cited above will be the central guide for modifying nonidentified models to bring about identification.

Armed with this rule, let us continue examining the aspiration model of Figure 11. Our basic objective is to identify equation 50 by imposing further zero restrictions on it. Clearly it would be inappropriate to increase the number of zero restrictions by deleting from the equation one or more of the explanatory variables already in it. Assuming that the original model was an accurate specification of an underlying theory about educational and occupational aspirations of male adolescents, deleting one of the variables from the equation—while keeping it in the other equations of the model—would lead to model *misspecification*, i.e., to a model inconsistent with the underlying theory. But by adding additional exogenous variables to the model which affect other variables in the model, *but not* X_3, we may be able to increase the number of zero restrictions in equation 50 sufficiently to achieve identification, without misspecifying the model.

For example, while respondent's intelligence (Z_5) is included in the model as an exogenous variable affecting respondent aspiration levels, we had assumed that an indicator of the intelligence level of the respondent's friend was unavailable. But if an indicator of friend's intelligence were available, we could include it in the model and assume that it has effects parallel to those of respondent's intelligence. In particular, we would assume that friend's intelligence (Z_8) has a direct effect on X_2 (friend's occupational aspiration level), and X_4 (friend's educational aspiration level) but no direct effect on either X_1 or X_3 (the aspiration levels for the respondent). With the addition of the new exogenous variable, our model takes the following form:

$$X_1 = \beta_{12}X_2 + \gamma_{15}Z_5 + \gamma_{16}Z_6 + \epsilon_1 \qquad \text{[61; same as 48]}$$

$$X_2 = \beta_{21}X_1 + \gamma_{27}Z_7 + \gamma_{28}Z_8 + \epsilon_2 \qquad \text{[62; modified 49]}$$

$$X_3 = \beta_{31}X_1 + \beta_{34}X_4 + \gamma_{35}Z_5 + \gamma_{36}Z_6 + \epsilon_3 \qquad \text{[63; same as 50]}$$

$$X_4 = \beta_{42}X_2 + \beta_{43}X_3 + \gamma_{47}Z_7 + \gamma_{48}Z_8 + \epsilon_4 \qquad \text{[64; modified 51]}$$

In this model, the structural equation for X_3 has one more zero restriction than it did previously. We have thus modified the aspiration model consistent with our rule of thumb about zero restrictions; it is hoped that the change is sufficient to identify the model. Indeed, an application of the algorithm shows that the model is now identified. More specifically, structural equations 61 and 62 are overidentified, while equations 63 and 64 are exactly identified.[24]

Let us also attempt to identify the voting behavior model of Figure 12. Again, there is only one underidentified structural equation in the model—equation 52, determining party ID. Thus, to identify the model we must seek exogenous variables that can be added to the model but *left out* of equation 52. Put differently, we must find at least one exogenous variable that we believe has no effect on party ID (X_1), but does have a direct effect on at least one other endogenous variable in the model. Here we can turn to Page and Jones's (1979) original research for guidance. They propose that an individual's "personal qualities evaluations" of candidates affects the individual's comparative candidate evaluations, but has no direct effect on party ID or policy/issue positions. They also hypothesize that income is a factor that has a direct causal effect on policy/issue positions, but no direct effect on party ID or candidate evaluations. If we add personal qualities evaluations (Z_7) and income (Z_8) as exogenous variables to the model to reflect these hypotheses, we obtain the following equations:

$$X_1 = \beta_{12}X_2 + \beta_{13}X_3 + \gamma_{14}Z_4 + \gamma_{15}Z_5 + \gamma_{16}Z_6 + \epsilon_1 \qquad \text{[65; same as 52]}$$

$$X_2 = \beta_{21}X_1 + \beta_{23}X_3 + \gamma_{26}Z_6 + \gamma_{27}Z_7 + \epsilon_2 \qquad \text{[66; modified 53]}$$

$$X_3 = \beta_{31}X_1 + \beta_{32}X_2 + \gamma_{34}Z_4 + \gamma_{38}Z_8 + \epsilon_3 \qquad \text{[67; modified 54]}$$

If we were to work through the steps of the algorithm, we would find that the voting behavior model is now identified.[25]

Thus, we have seen that adding exogenous variables to a nonidentified multiequation model can be used to achieve identification. Of course, arbitrarily adding exogenous variables to a model will not be helpful. The illustrations we examined suggest that two types of requirements must guide the addition of exogenous variables to a nonidentified model—some technical, some theoretical. At a technical level, to identify an underidentified equation in a model, one or more exogenous variables must be added to other equations that are not added to the equation of interest. But not all causal positionings of these new variables in a model will sufficiently restrict the model so that the equation becomes identified. Also, there is no simple rule to guide the positioning of these variables; one must experiment with different positionings and test the new equation using the algorithm.[26]

These technical requirements make overcoming underidentification sound like a game in which we "shuffle" around new exogenous variables until we find something that works; but this would be a poor strategy. As with all methodological strategies, if it is to be used effectively and appropriately, the addition of exogenous variables must be done keeping theory in mind. For example, adding the variable Personal Qualities Evaluations (Z_7) to the voting behavior model of Figure 12 (to produce the model of equations 65 through 67) is only reasonable if we have confidence, based on our theory, that Z_7 has no *direct* causal impact on Party ID (X_1) or Policy/Issue Positions (X_3), and thus that any effect Z_7 has on X_1 or X_3 is *indirect* through Z_7's effect on Comparative Candidate Evaluation (X_2). Even this, however, does not suffice. We must also believe, based on theory, that Z_7 has a substantial impact on X_2. Klein (1962: 18) states this warning very well:

Identification cannot be cheaply achieved in any particular investigation by simply adding some weak or marginal variables to the relationships of a system. One must add something substantial and significant which had been previously neglected.

Assume, for instance, that Personal Qualities Evaluations (Z_7) has a very weak effect on Comparative Candidate Evaluation (X_2), i.e., that a substantial change in the value of Z_7 produces only a very small change in the value of X_2. Then, while the revised voting behavior model will be identified, the model will be of little value in estimating the true parameters of the model. This is because when the exogenous variables in a nonrecursive model are only weakly related to the endogenous variables in the model, the statistical techniques available to estimate parameters will produce estimates with large standard errors. This implies that confidence intervals for the parameters will be very wide; thus our empirical analysis will not give us the ability to measure the magnitude of causal effects with any reasonable degree of precision.

Finally, the vital role of theory in identifying a model suggests that testing models for identification must be done early in the research process, rather than as an afterthought when an initial model proves nonidentified. If the search for exogenous variables sufficient to identify a model fails to be carried out when a research project is being designed, and *prior* to the collection of data, one can easily be left in the awkward position of having no data for the exogenous variables that are theoretically appropriate and technically necessary for identifying the model. In such a case, successfully modifying a nonidentified model to achieve identification will be small comfort indeed.

5. ESTIMATION TECHNIQUES

In this chapter, we will examine procedures through which parameters for the equations of nonrecursive models can be appropriately estimated. We will, of course, assume throughout this chapter that we are working with an identified model, as nonidentification makes it so that reasonable parameter estimates cannot be determined. Chapter 1 notes that ordinary least squares regression analysis generates unbiased and consistent parameter estimators when applied to the equations of a *recursive* model. We will see that even when a *nonrecursive* model is identified, OLS regression is inappropriate, as it produces biased and inconsistent estimators. Fortunately, the OLS procedure can be modified to develop techniques that, when applied to nonrecursive models, generate parameter estimators that may be biased but are at least consistent.

The reason OLS regression is no longer appropriate when we move from the recursive to the nonrecursive case is our inability in the latter to make assumptions that guarantee that each error term, ϵ_i, is uncorrelated with all explanatory variables in the structural equation including ϵ_i. Unless the error term in an equation is uncorrelated with all explanatory variables in the equation, the OLS estimators for its parameters will be biased and inconsistent. To illustrate this, consider a two-variable regression model of the form

$$Y = \beta X + \epsilon \qquad [68]$$

where we assume that X, Y, and ϵ all have mean zero, but where we make no assumption that the error term, ϵ, is uncorrelated with the explanatory variable X. If we multiply through equation 68 by X we get

$$XY = \beta X^2 + X\epsilon \qquad [69]$$

Then, taking expectations of both sides yields

$$E(XY) = \beta E(X^2) + E(X\epsilon) \qquad [70]$$

But $E(XY) = cov(X, Y)$, $E(X\epsilon) = cov(X, \epsilon)$, and $E(X^2) = var(X)$.[27] Thus equation 70 can be written as

$$cov(X, Y) = [\beta var(X)] + cov(X, \epsilon) \qquad [71]$$

or, equivalently, as

$$\beta = \frac{cov(X, Y) - cov(X, \epsilon)}{var(X)} = \frac{cov(X, Y)}{var(X)} - \frac{cov(X, \epsilon)}{var(X)} \qquad [72]$$

This means that the parameter β is a function of two covariances—that between X and Y, and that between X and ϵ. If we were to estimate β with the OLS estimator $\hat{\beta}^\circ$ given by

$$\hat{\beta}^\circ = \frac{S_{YX}}{S_X^2}$$

we would obtain a *biased* estimator; in essence, the OLS estimator of β estimates just the "cov(X,Y) / var(X)" portion of β, and is insensitive to the "cov(X,ϵ) / var(X)" component. Thus, as an estimator of β, $\hat{\beta}^\circ$ is biased by an amount proportional to the extent to which the explanatory variable and the error term in equation 68 covary.

In this chapter I will present two limited-information techniques appropriate for nonrecursive models: (1) indirect least squares (ILS) and (2) two-stage least squares (2SLS). These limited information techniques estimate the parameters of a nonrecursive model one equation at a time and based exclusively on the restrictions imposed on the single equation being estimated. Indeed, both ILS and 2SLS are straightforward modifications of the most common limited information technique—OLS regression. Also, both techniques—when applied appropriately to nonrecursive models—yield parameter estimators that are consistent.

In addition to the limited-information techniques, there are several *full-information* estimation techniques appropriate for nonrecursive models. These techniques estimate the parameters for all equations in a model simultaneously, using information about the restrictions imposed on all equations. The advantage of full-information parameter estimators is that they are more efficient than those generated by limited-information techniques.[28] On the other hand, full-information techniques are not as widely available as limited-information ones in social science computer statistical packages and, when available, are much more expensive to run. Furthermore, in addition to these practical limitations, full-information estimators seem to be more sensitive to errors in model specification than limited-information estimators, as biases in estimators resulting from specification error in one equation tend to be transmitted through parameter estimators for all the equations in a model. For these reasons, full-information techniques are used only rarely in social science research, and I will focus in this paper on the limited-information approaches.[29]

Indirect Least Squares and Exactly Identified Equations

Indirect least squares (ILS) is a technique that can appropriately be used to estimate the parameters of exactly identified equations in a nonrecursive model. The technique is a straightforward extension of the procedure by which models are tested for identification using the reduced-form perspective. To see this, let us reconsider the protest violence model of Figure 8, which was examined from the reduced-form perspective in Chapter 2. In the earlier analysis, we began by converting the structural equations of the model (equations 22 and 23) to reduced-form equations 27 and 28. We then demonstrated that structural equation 22 was identified by showing that knowledge of the reduced-form parameters (π_{13}, π_{14}, π_{23}, and π_{24}) would uniquely determine the structural parameters β_{12} and γ_{13} of equation 22. The structural parameters would be determined because equalities 29.1 through 29.6 could be solved—treating the reduced-form parameters as knowns—to give

$$\beta_{12} = \pi_{14}/\pi_{24} \tag{73}$$

and

$$\gamma_{13} = \pi_{13} - (\pi_{14}\pi_{23}/\pi_{24}) \tag{74}$$

Of course, in practice, the true reduced-form parameters will rarely be known; thus, we will generally not be able to solve for the true structural parameters. But we saw that the reduced-form equations for a nonrecursive model will always be identified. Furthermore, the explanatory variables on the right-hand side of a reduced-form equation will all be exogenous and, by the assumptions of the model, will all be uncorrelated with the error term in the equation. Therefore, while we will rarely know the true reduced-form parameters, we will always be able to apply OLS regression to obtain unbiased estimates of the reduced-form parameters. For the protest violence model, we could obtain OLS estimates of the reduced-form parameters, which can be denoted $\hat{\pi}_{12}$, $\hat{\pi}_{14}$, $\hat{\pi}_{23}$, and $\hat{\pi}_{24}$. Then these estimates could be substituted for their respective parameters in equations 73 and 74 to yield:

$$\hat{\beta}_{12} = \hat{\pi}_{14}/\hat{\pi}_{24} \tag{75}$$

and

$$\hat{\gamma}_{13} = \hat{\pi}_{13} - (\hat{\pi}_{14}\hat{\pi}_{23}/\hat{\pi}_{24}) \tag{76}$$

Finally, performing the operations on the right-hand side of these equations would produce estimates for the structural parameters β_{12} and γ_{13}.

The procedure just outlined is called indirect least squares, as it employs ordinary least squares regression in an "indirect" fashion to obtain estimates for structural parameters. The general steps in the procedure are as follows. First, the structural equations of a nonrecursive model are placed in reduced form. Second, OLS regression is used to obtain unbiased estimates for the parameters of the reduced-form equations. Then, if a structural equation in the model is exactly identified, it will be possible to substitute the reduced-form OLS parameter estimates in the equations comparable to 29.1 through 29.6, and solve the equations for unique estimates of the equation's structural parameters.

While the OLS estimators for the reduced-form parameters are unbiased, unfortunately, the final ILS structural parameter estimators are not. The reason is that the structual parameter estimators will generally be nonlinear transformations of the reduced-form parameter estimators, and nonlinear transformations of unbiased estimators will not in general be unbiased. This is the case with the ILS estimators for equation 22 of the protest violence model, as equations 75 and 76 show that $\hat{\beta}_{12}$ and $\hat{\gamma}_{13}$ are obtained through operations requiring multiplying or dividing one reduced-form parameter estimate by another. But while ILS estimators are biased, they are at least *consistent*. Thus, as the sample size approaches infinity, an ILS estimate will approach being "on target." However, the fact that ILS estimators are only consistent, and not unbiased, suggests the importance of a large sample for accurate estimation, as there is no general guarantee that the expected value of an ILS estimator generated by a small sample will be "close" in value to the true population parameter.

The beauty of estimation by ILS is the simplicity of its underlying logic. It is a natural extension of the reduced-form perspective for testing a model for identification and, thus, can be easily understood. But just as we found the computations in the reduced-form perspective too difficult to perform in a practical sense in all but the most simple of nonrecursive models, ILS in practice will also generally prove too tedious to be useful. While the step of ILS requiring OLS regression analysis on reduced-form equations can be performed using any of a variety of computer statistical packages, these packages generally will not perform the final step of solving for the structural parameter estimates. Fortunately, an alternative estimation technique, two-stage least squares (2SLS), is available in some statistical packages; and 2SLS can be used to estimate the structural parameters of an exactly identified equation in a nonrecursive model. Furthermore, for an exactly identified equation, 2SLS yields parameter estimates identical to those generated by ILS.

But our earlier analysis of the identification problem from the reduced-form perspective should alert us that ILS poses a problem when estimating parameters for an overidentified equation. For example, we saw that equation 31 in the occupational aspiration model of Figure 9 is overidentified; using the procedure that we now refer to as ILS, we found two different expressions for estimating β_{21}:

$$\hat{\beta}'_{21} = \hat{\pi}_{23}/\hat{\pi}_{13}$$

and

$$\hat{\beta}''_{21} = \hat{\pi}_{24}/\hat{\pi}_{14}$$

Indeed, this illustrates the general problem; when applied to an over-identified equation, ILS yields multiple expressions for estimating the structural parameters of the equation, which—because of sampling error—generate different estimates for the same parameter. Note, however, that while we have two estimators for β_{21} ($\hat{\beta}_{21}'$ and $\hat{\beta}_{21}''$), *both* of the estimators are consistent. Thus, as the sample size for estimation approaches infinity, both $\hat{\beta}_{21}'$ and $\hat{\beta}_{21}''$ approach the parameter β_{21}'s true value, and the difference between the values of $\hat{\beta}_{21}'$ and $\hat{\beta}_{21}''$ becomes negligible. Of course, infinitely large samples are unavailable; thus, we are faced with multiple ILS estimates of the structural parameters of an overidentified equation. Clearly, if we could devise an appropriate procedure for "combining" these multiple estimates, we should be able to obtain a better estimate of an equation's structural parameters. In essence, 2SLS is a technique that does just this.

Two-Stage Least Squares

A different modification of OLS regression analysis yields another limited-information technique appropriate for estimating parameters of nonrecursive models. This technique also involves estimating the parameters of the reduced-form equations for a model as a preliminary step toward estimating the structural parameters. Unlike ILS, however, 2SLS generates unique estimates for the parameters of overidentified as well as exactly identified equations. In the case of an exactly identified equation, 2SLS yields estimates identical to those generated by ILS. Furthermore, if all equations in a nonrecursive model are exactly identified, the estimates determined by 2SLS and ILS will be equivalent to the estimates generated by the full-information estimation techniques, which are beyond the scope of this paper.

To develop the procedures involved in 2SLS estimation, we will examine further structural equation 31 in the occupational aspiration model of Figure 9. The application of ILS to this overidentified equation left us with multiple estimates for its parameters and the need to resolve the differences between these estimates to yield a single estimate for each of the parameters—β_{21} and γ_{25} —in the equation.

The starting point for 2SLS is a recognition of why OLS regression is inappropriate for equation 31. The reason is that there is no assumption in the model that X_1 is uncorrelated with the equation's error term, ϵ_2. Given this, the idea behind 2SLS is to find a *modified* variable *similar to* X_1, but which is *uncorrelated with* ϵ_2, so that this variable can be substituted for X_1 in equation 31, thus allowing OLS to be appropriately used on the revised equation. How is this idea implemented? As the name of the technique suggests, there are two stages in the 2SLS procedure.

In the first stage, we use OLS regression to estimate the parameters for the reduced-form equation for X_1—equation 34. An alternative, but equivalent, way of thinking about this is that the first stage involves regressing X_1 on all exogenous variables in the model—in this case, Z_3, Z_4, and Z_5. This gives us the OLS reduced-form parameters estimates for equation 34, which we can call $\hat{\pi}_{13}$, $\hat{\pi}_{14}$, and $\hat{\pi}_{15}$. Then we can use these estimates and the equation

$$\hat{X}_1 = \hat{\pi}_{13}Z_3 + \hat{\pi}_{14}Z_4 + \hat{\pi}_{15}Z_5 \qquad [77]$$

to construct a new variable $\hat{X}_1$, typically referred to as an *instrumental variable* for X_1. $\hat{X}_1$ has two important properties. First, it is "similar" to X_1. Indeed, it is the "most similar" variable to X_1 that can be obtained by taking a linear combination of the exogenous variables in the model. Second, $\hat{X}_1$ is uncorrelated with the error term, ϵ_2, of equation 31. This is true since, by assumption, Z_3, Z_4, and Z_5 are uncorrelated with ϵ_2, and X_1 is just a linear combination of these three variables.

In the second stage of 2SLS, we substitute the instrumental variable $\hat{X}_1$ for X_1 in equation 31 to get

$$X_2 = \beta_{21}^t \hat{X}_1 + \gamma_{25}^t Z_5 + \epsilon_2 \qquad [78]$$

(where we use the superscript "t" to distinguish the parameters in this equation from those in equation 31). But, since we know that both Z_5 and $\hat{X}_1$ are uncorrelated with ϵ_2, it is appropriate to use OLS regression to estimate the coefficients of equation 78. The values obtained—$\hat{\beta}_{21}^t$, and $\hat{\gamma}_{25}^t$—are the 2SLS estimates for the structural coefficients β_{21} and γ_{25} of equation 31. In a sense, then, $\hat{X}_1$ is used as an instrument to allow us to estimate the parameters of the original structural equation.

We can generalize this procedure to arrive at the basic steps in 2SLS estimation. First, OLS regression analysis is used to estimate the parameters of each reduced-form equation for the model. Operationally, this requires regressing separately each endogenous variable in the model ($X_1, X_2, \ldots, X_m$) on all exogenous variables in the model ($Z_{m+1}, Z_{m+2}, \ldots, Z_{m+k}$). Put differently, we are regressing each endogenous variable on all variables in the model assumed to be uncorrelated with the model's error term. Then we use the OLS parameter estimates obtained and data for the exogenous variables to construct instrumental variables $\hat{X}_1, \hat{X}_2, \ldots, \hat{X}_m$—each of which can be assumed uncorrelated with all error terms in the model. In a sense, the reason we use all (as opposed to some) exogenous variables as independent variables in these first-stage regressions is because we want to construct instrumental variables as similar to the endogenous variables as possible while still making certain that the new variables are uncorrelated with the error terms in the equations. The larger is the number of exogenous variables we include as independent variables in the first-stage regressions, the closer are the instrumental variables to the original endogenous variables.

In the next step of 2SLS, any endogenous variable, X_j, serving as an explanatory variable in one of the structural equations, is replaced by the corresponding instrumental variable, $\hat{X}_j$. Given these substitutions, each explanatory variable in the modified structural equations can be assumed uncorrelated with the error terms in the model. Thus, it is appropriate, as the final step in 2SLS, to use OLS regression to estimate the parameters of the revised structural equations. The resulting estimates are the 2SLS estimates for the original structural equations.

2SLS can be applied to estimate the structural parameters of *any* overidentified equation in a nonrecursive model. Furthermore, 2SLS can also be appropriately used with exactly identified equations; and with such equations the estimates generated are identical to those determined by ILS. Thus, the most common strategy when estimating the coefficients of a nonrecursive model is to use 2SLS on all equations of the model.

The estimators generated by 2SLS (like those from ILS) may be biased, but are consistent. Unfortunately, the small-sample properties of the estimates are not as clear. However, there is some evidence from Monte Carlo simulation studies that with small samples 2SLS estimators for nonrecursive models are less biased than OLS estimators for the same parameters (Namboodiri et al., 1975: 519). On the other hand, 2SLS estimators seem to have larger standard errors than OLS parameter estimators (Namboodiri et al., 1975: 519). But the size of the standard errors of 2SLS estimators is partially a function of the degree to which the instrumental variables created in the first stage are similar to the endogenous variables they replace. Ceteris paribus, the higher the correlation between the instrumental variables and the original endogenous variables, the more efficient the parameter estimates produced by 2SLS. This again sensitizes us to the fact it is not helpful to add to a model exogenous variables that are only weakly related to the endogenous variables for the purpose of achieving identification. While the resulting model may, technically, be identified, the instrumental variables created in 2SLS will have low correlations with the model's endogenous variables, and the estimators of the structural parameters will have large standard errors, thereby giving us little confidence that we have accurately estimated the model's true parameters.

As described, 2SLS is a procedure involving two separate stages of OLS regression analysis. For this reason, 2SLS can be performed using any computer program or statistical package that allows the "predicted values" of the dependent variable from a regression to be "stored" and used in succeeding regression analyses (e.g., the regression procedure in SPSS-X). However, the computation of 2SLS estimates does not really have to be done in two separate stages. A matrix-algebra formula has been devised, which can be used to compute the estimates in a single step, and several common statistical packages (such as SAS and BMD) use this formula to calculate 2SLS estimates.

Indeed, this one-step procedure is preferable to the two-step approach for reasons beyond computational ease. While both methods of applying 2SLS yield the same, correct, *unstandardized* estimates of structural parameters, the two-step process may yield *standardized* parameter estimates that are incorrect. More precisely, the standardized estimates for exogenous variables produced by the two-step approach will be correct and match those produced by the single-step approach. However, the standardized parameter estimates for endogenous explanatory variables will be attenuated, i.e., less than the correct estimates generated by the single-step approach. The estimates are attenuated because the variance of the instrumental variables created in the first stage of 2SLS are less than those of the original endogenous variables. This reduced variance serves to attenuate the value of the standardized parameter estimates obtained in the second-stage regression (Kritzer, 1976).

Fortunately, Kritzer, identifies several ways of correction for the attenuation. First, the variables in the model can be standardized *before* beginning the two-step regression procedure. With the preliminary standardization, the standardized estimates generated by the two-step procedure will no longer be attenuated. Second, the attenuated parameter estimate for an instrumental variable can be corrected after the two-step procedure has been performed by dividing the parameter estimate by the multiple correlation coefficient (R) for the first-stage regression used to create the instrumental variable. But again, these methods of correction for attenuation are needed only when standardized parameter estimates are being calculated; the two-step procedure will give accurate 2SLS estimates for unstandardized parameter estimates without any correction being necessary. Of course, Blalock (1967), Achen (1977), and others argue that only in rare situations is there a legitimate need to report standardized parameter estimates. For this reason, the best way to avoid attenuation in the parameter estimates for endogenous variables when using a two-step approach for calculating 2SLS estimates is to calculate unstandardized coefficients in the first place.

But there is another, more important, reason why it is better to use a program that calculates 2SLS estimates using the one-step matrix algebra calculation formula. While the two-step approach yields accurate unstandardized parameter estimates (and correctable standardized estimates), it produces *incorrect* standard errors and multiple R^2 values. With the computer programs and statistical packages designed explicitly to do 2SLS, standard errors and R^2 values are calculated appropriately, on the basis of the observed values of the *original* explanatory variables in the model. However, when 2SLS estimates are determined through a two-step procedure, the only standard errors and R^2 values obtained for the estimates are the ones for the second-stage OLS regressions. These standard errors are calculated on the basis of the observed values of the *instrumental* variables (rather than the original explanatory variables), and are not the correct standard errors for the final 2SLS parameter estimates. Thus, whenever possible, one should calculate 2SLS parameter estimates using a computer program or package explicitly designed to do 2SLS, thus yielding (1) correct standardized and unstandardized parameter estimates and (2) correct standard errors and R^2 values. The most widely available statistical packages containing the 2SLS procedure are SAS (Statistical Analysis System) and TSP (Time Series Processor), but other packages include SHAZAM, B345, and QUAIL.

Two-Stage Least Squares and the
Multicollinearity Problem

We have seen that 2SLS can be appropriately used to generate parameter estimates for exactly identified and overidentified structural equations in a nonrecursive model. Perhaps some readers—still clinging to the notion that underidentification can be overcome if "only the right statistical technique were devised"— might try applying 2SLS to an underidentified equation. This strategy will not work; in fact, in some (but not all) cases, the 2SLS technique will "break down" with under-identified equations due to multicollinearity. For example, consider equation 23 in the protest violence model of Figure 8—an equation we have verified was underidentified. If we were to apply the 2SLS proce-dure to equation 23, we would begin by regressing the endogenous explanatory variable in the equation, X_1, on the exogenous variables in the model, Z_3 and Z_4, to create the instrumental variable, $\hat{X}_1$. So far, this would work fine. But in the second stage, we would substitute $\hat{X}_1$ for X_1 in equation 23 and obtain

$$X_2 = \beta_{21}^t \hat{X}_1 + \gamma_{23}^t Z_3 + \gamma_{24}^t Z_4 + \epsilon_2 \qquad [79]$$

And at this point, the technique would collapse. Since the instrumental variable $\hat{X}_1$ is a linear combination of Z_3 and Z_4, equation 79 is character-ized by *perfect* multicollinearity; if $\hat{X}_1$ were regressed on Z_3 and Z_4, R^2 would equal 1.00 precisely. When perfect multicollinearity is present, OLS regression will fail to yield a unique set of parameter estimates; instead, there will be an infinite number of sets of parameter estimates consistent with the data at hand.[30] Again we are left with the same conclusion; statistical procedures cannot be used to obtain meaningful parameter estimates for underidentified equations.

Multicollinearity, in less extreme forms, is also often a problem when 2SLS is applied to identified equations. This occurs because the instru-mental variables created in the first-stage regressions will always be more highly correlated with the exogenous variables in a model than the original endogenous variables they replace. For example, in estimating the parameters of the occupational aspiration model of Figure 9, the correlation between $\hat{X}_1$ and Z_5 (see equation 78) will necessarily be greater than the correlation between X_1 and Z_5, since $\hat{X}_1$ was created by regressing X_1 on a set of exogenous variables *including* Z_5. Indeed, since each instrumental variable created for 2SLS is a linear combination of the full set of exogenous variables in the model, in general, the greater the percentage of exogenous variables from a model which are included as explanatory variables in a given structural equation, the more likely it it that high multicollinearity will characterize 2SLS estimation.

When high multicollinearity is present in 2SLS estimation, detecting its presence is not difficult. A detailed discussion of detection techniques is beyond the scope of this paper, but good treatments are available elsewhere (see, e.g., Lewis-Beck, 1980: 58-63; Hanushek and Jackson, 1977: 86-93). An important point to remember when employing 2SLS is that it is not sufficient to test for multicollinearity among the original explanatory variables in a structural equation. In many cases, although there may not be significant multicollinearity among the original explanatory variables, there will be high multicollinearity in the second-stage regressions involving the instrumental variables.

Note that even when high multicollinearity is present, the parameters determined by 2SLS will still be consistent; the major consequence of high multicollinearity is large standard errors (thus, wide confidence intervals) for parameter estimates (Hanushek and Jackson, 1977: 86-90). The only ideal strategy for overcoming high multicollinearity is to obtain more data; an increase in sample size will tend to reduce the standard errors of parameter estimates, thus offsetting the effect of multicollinearity.

Another common strategy for dealing with multicollinearity is to delete the variable that is causing the problem from the equation. Since, in the context of 2SLS, it is generally the instrumental variables that cause the problem, this would usually mean deleting one or more endogenous variables from the explanatory variables in a structural equation, which would be equivalent to assuming that the associated structural parameters are equal to zero. This is hardly an ideal strategy, as the resulting model would misspecify the theory underlying the model, and the 2SLS estimates would no longer be consistent.

Finally, some have recommended the use of a technique called *ridge regression* for estimating the parameters of a regression model in the face of high multicollinearity (see, e.g., Hoerl and Kennard, 1970; Deegan, 1975). This technique is beyond the scope of this paper. Furthermore, the implications of using ridge (instead of OLS) regression in the final step of 2SLS have not yet been clarified.[31] Kritzer (1976: 89) sums up the situation with respect to multicollinearity well: "the user of 2SLS needs to be sensitive to potential multicollinearity problems, but if such problems arise, the options available to the user are limited."[32]

Parameter Estimation in the Occupational and Educational Aspiration Model

To illustrate 2SLS, we will apply the technique to estimate the parameters of the aspiration model of equations 61 through 64. We saw in Chapter 4 that this model is identified; in particular, equations 63 and 64 are exactly identified, while equations 61 and 62 are overidentified. Consequently, the parameters of equations 63 and 64 can be estimated using ILS or 2SLS; but only 2SLS can be used with equations 61 and 62.

However, computationally, it is easier to use a computer statistical package to estimate parameters for all four equations using 2SLS. The data set used for estimation is that originally collected by Duncan et al. (1971), and consists of interview and testing information for 329 male adolescents.[33]

Estimation for this model by 2SLS could be done by regressing each of the four endogenous variables in the model—X_1, X_2, X_3, and X_4—on all exogenous variables in the model (Z_5, Z_6, Z_7, and Z_8) to create four instrumental variables—$\hat{X}_1$, $\hat{X}_2$, $\hat{X}_3$, and $\hat{X}_4$. Then these instrumental variables could be substituted for the corresponding endogenous explanatory variables in equations 61 through 64, and OLS regression could be used to estimate the parameters for the revised equations. The estimates obtained would be the 2SLS estimates we were seeking. It is preferable, however, to use a computer program specially designed for 2SLS, thus allowing us to calculate accurate standard errors for our parameter estimates.

Table 1 contains unstandardized 2SLS parameter estimates for the model along with their standard errors. The parameters for equations 61 through 64 were also estimated using OLS regression on each equation. Although we know that OLS is inappropriate for nonrecursive models, I have included these estimates in Table 1 to illustrate the differences between the 2SLS and OLS estimates. (In the following discussion, OLS estimates are denoted with the superscript "o," and 2SLS estimates have superscript "t.")

We can note that for some parameters in the aspiration model, the OLS estimate does not differ that much in value from the 2SLS estimate. But for a few parameters, the differences are dramatic. Indeed, there are three parameters for which the 2SLS estimate is less than half the size of the OLS estimate: $\hat{\gamma}_{48}^{t} = .14$, while $\hat{\gamma}_{48}^{o} = .50$; $\hat{\beta}_{31}^{t} = .19$, while $\hat{\beta}_{31}^{o} = .46$; and $\hat{\gamma}_{47}^{t} = .17$, while $\hat{\gamma}_{47}^{o} = .35$. Thus, the statistical results for the aspiration model illustrate that OLS regression can give results that differ widely from the consistent parameter estimates generated by 2SLS. Note also that the estimates for this model reflect the typical pattern in which the standard errors of 2SLS parameter estimates are larger than those of OLS estimates. Indeed, for all parameters in the aspiration model, the 2SLS standard error is greater than or equal to the OLS standard error.

The combination of differing parameter estimates *and* differing standard errors from one estimation technique to the other dramatically changes the substantive interpretations that we would draw if we were to shift from OLS to the more appropriate 2SLS. For example, the OLS results suggest that Friend's Intelligence Level (Z_8) has a statistically significant effect on Friend's Educational Aspiration Level (X_4), as

TABLE 1
Parameter Estimates for the Occupational and Educational
Aspiration Model of Equations 61 Through 64

Explanatory Variable	Structural Parameter	Unstandardized Estimates of Parameters (with standard errors in parentheses)	
		2SLS	OLS
Equation 61			
X_2	β_{12}	.40 (.10)	.30 (.05)
Z_5	γ_{15}	.65 (.12)	.70 (.12)
Z_6	γ_{16}	.35 (.12)	.41 (.11)
Equation 62			
X_1	β_{21}	.34 (.12)	.26 (.05)
Z_7	γ_{27}	.35 (.12)	.39 (.11)
Z_8	γ_{28}	.82 (.13)	.87 (.11)
Equation 63			
X_1	β_{31}	.19 (.70)	.46 (.05)
X_4	β_{34}	.20 (.30)	.12 (.05)
Z_5	γ_{35}	.50 (.46)	.32 (.11)
Z_6	γ_{36}	.53 (.26)	.43 (.10)
Equation 64			
X_2	β_{42}	.77 (1.23)	.42 (.05)
X_3	β_{43}	.11 (.40)	.12 (.04)
Z_7	γ_{47}	.17 (.51)	.35 (.09)
Z_8	γ_{48}	.14 (1.04)	.50 (.10)

$\hat{\gamma}_{48}^{\circ} = .50$ is five times the size of its standard error (.10). In contrast, the 2SLS results indicate the effect of Friend's Intelligence on Friend's Educational Aspiration to be much less substantial ($\hat{\gamma}_{48}^{t} = .14$), and not significantly different from zero at customary levels of significance; in fact, the 2SLS parameter estimate of .14 is less than 20% of the size of its standard error (1.04).

The large size of the standard errors for some equations in the aspiration model gives reason to suspect that multicollinearity may be a problem. The most commonly used technique to detect multicollinearity is the inspection of *bivariate* correlations for all pairs of independent variables in the equation. But, while high multicollinearity may at times be reflected in the bivariate correlations among the independent variables, in general, high multicollinearity can be present without a pattern of high bivariate correlations. A preferable test for detecting multicollinearity in an equation is to examine a set of *multiple* correlations—in particular, the multiple R^2 value for each independent variable in the equation when regressed on all other independent variables in the equation (see Lemieux, 1978). We can denote these multiple correlations by R_j^2, which represents the multiple R^2 coefficient when the independent variable (X_j or Z_j) is regressed on all other independent variables in the equation, and by R_j^2, which denotes the multiple R^2 coefficient when the instrumental variable $\hat{X}_j$ is regressed on all other independent variables in a second-stage regression in 2SLS.

Using this test demonstrates that multicollinearity is not present in an extreme amount when estimating the parameters of equations 61 through 62 using 2SLS. In the second-stage regressions for equation 61, the largest R_j^2 value is $R_2^2 = .37$, while for equation 62, the largest R_j^2 value is $R_1^2 = .51$. On the other hand, the second-stage regressions for estimating the parameters of equations 63 and 64 are characterized by extremely high multicollinearity. For equation 63, when we regress the instrumental variable for either X_1 or X_4 on the explanatory variables in the second-stage regression for 2SLS, we obtain multiple R^2 values—R_1^2 and R_4^2—exceeding .98. In this case, the high multicollinearity is due principally to the large correlation between the two instrumental variables—$\hat{X}_4$ and $\hat{X}_1$—in the second-stage regression equation [$r_{\hat{X}_1 \hat{X}_4} = .87$]. Similarly, for equation 64, regressing either instrumental variable, $\hat{X}_2$ or $\hat{X}_3$, on the other explanatory variables in the second-stage regression equation generates an R^2 value (R_2^2 or R_3^2) greater than .96.

It is interesting to note that the extensive multicollinearity present in these two equations in the second-stage regressions for 2SLS is not present among the explanatory variables in the original equations. For example, in contrast to an R_4^2 value of .99 in the second-stage regression for estimating the parameters of equation 63, regressing the original variable X_4 on the other explanatory variables in equation 63 gives an R^2 value of only .17. This then is a graphic illustration that it is not sufficient to test for multicollinearity among the *original* explanatory variables in a structural equation when using 2SLS. Multicollinearity among the original variables can be quite low even when high multicollinearity is present after substituting instrumental variables for the endogenous explanatory variables.

Having detected a multicollinearity problem in the 2SLS estimation, there is little one can do at this stage of the analysis to overcome the problem. The best strategy for overcoming multicollinearity would be to broaden the amount of information available by increasing the sample size. A sample of 329 is fairly small, and increasing it substantially could ease the multicollinearity problem and yield 2SLS parameter estimates with smaller standard errors. Of course, the fact that we are working with a fixed data set for this illustration eliminates the option of increasing the sample size. Another possibility would be to delete certain explanatory variables from some of the structural equations. Certainly, deleting either X_1 or X_4 from equation 63 *and* either X_2 or X_3 from equation 64 would greatly reduce the magnitude of multicollinearity in the 2SLS estimation. However, the reduction in multicollinearity would come at the expense of grossly misspecifying the aspiration model. Deleting these variables would require an assumption that either (1) occupational aspirations are not a cause of educational aspirations, or (2) one's educational aspirations are unaffected by those of one's peer. Both of these assumptions are at odds with the theory underlying the empirical analysis.

Given these constraints, we must accept that the data available are not sufficient to provide estimates of the parameters of equations 63 and 64 in which we can place a great deal of confidence. The extreme multicollinearity in the second-stage regressions for 2SLS makes it so that the parameter estimates obtained would tend to fluctuate considerably from one sample to another. On the other hand, high multicollinearity is not present in estimating the parameters of equations 61 and 62. Thus, despite the limitations of our data, we can derive useful estimates of the effects of the variables in the model on occupational aspirations. In particular, we have strong support for the hypothesis that there is reciprocal causation between the occupational aspirations of a male adolescent and those of a peer.

A Revised Protest Violence Model

For a second example of estimation using 2SLS, we will expand the model of Figure 8 to consider Kritzer's (1977) original model of the outbreak of violence at protest events. This model is diagramed in Figure 14 and represented formally by the following equations:

$$X_1 = \beta_{12}X_2 + \beta_{15}X_5 + \gamma_{19}Z_9 + \epsilon_1 \tag{80}$$

$$X_2 = \beta_{21}X_1 + \gamma_{23}Z_3 + \gamma_{24}Z_4 + \gamma_{26}Z_6 + \gamma_{27}Z_7 + \gamma_{28}Z_8 + \epsilon_2 \tag{81}$$

$$X_5 = \beta_{51}X_1 + \gamma_{53}Z_3 + \epsilon_5. \tag{82}$$

X_1, X_2, Z_3 and Z_4 are defined as in the model of Figure 8. However, an additional endogenous variable is added to the model (X_5) which represents the nature of arrests made at the protest. Kritzer hypothesizes that the nature of arrests is a factor affecting the level of violence of protestors (X_1), but that the level of protestor violence, in turn, affects the nature of arrests. In addition, several other exogenous variables have been added to the model, some of which are necessary to achieve identification. Three of these variables are thought to have direct effects only on X_2 (the level of violence of police): the use by protestors of obscene gestures (Z_6), the use by protestors of verbal obscenities (Z_7), and the type and number of police present (Z_8). Finally, one exogenous variable added—the degree of commitment of protestors to nonviolence (Z_9)—is hypothesized to have a direct effect only on X_1.

The use of the rank-condition algorithm shows that equation 81 of the revised protest violence model is exactly identified, while equations 80 and 82 are overidentified.[34] Thus, given adequate data, we can obtain meaningful estimates for the model's parameters using 2SLS. The data set I employed is that originally collected by Kritzer and consists of observations for a sample of 126 protest demonstrations.[35]

For this illustration, I have calculated standardized parameter estimates to illustrate that 2SLS estimates can be represented in either standardized or unstandardized form. As with the earlier illustration, Table 2 presents the 2SLS parameter estimates along with OLS estimates for comparison.[36] Just as with the earlier illustration, some of the OLS parameter estimates are quite different than their more appropriate 2SLS counterparts. The most dramatic difference is for β_{15}; here the 2SLS estimate is $-.45$, while the OLS estimate is oppositely signed at $.39$.[37] But the two estimates for β_{12} differ in value substantially as well, as $\hat{\beta}_{12}{}^t = 1.54$ while $\hat{\beta}_{12}{}^\circ = .36$. Also, the pattern of larger standard errors for OLS estimates than 2SLS estimates continues to hold; for all parameters in the protest violence model, the standard error of the 2SLS estimate is greater than or equal to that of the OLS estimate.

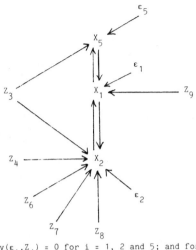

Assumptions: (i) $\text{cov}(\varepsilon_i, Z_j) = 0$ for $i = 1$, 2 and 5; and for $j = 3$, 4, 6, 7, 8 and 9

(ii) $E(X_i) = E(\varepsilon_i) = E(Z_j) = 0$ for $i = 1$, 2 and 5; and for $j = 3$, 4, 6, 7, 8 and 9

Notation: X_1 -- the Level of Violence of Protestors

X_2 -- the Level of Violence of Police

Z_3 -- the Nature of Civil Disobedience Committed by Protestors

Z_4 -- the Extent to Which Heavy Policy Equipment is Available

X_5 -- the Nature of Arrests Made at the Protest

Z_6 -- the Use of Obscene Gestures by Protestors

Z_7 -- the Use of Verbal Obscenities by Protestors

Z_8 -- the Type and Number of Police Present

Z_9 -- the Degree of Commitment of Protestors to Nonviolence

Figure 14: A Causal Diagram of the Nonrecursive Model of Equations 80 through 82

An examination of R_j^2 coefficients shows that multicollinearity is not sufficiently strong to warrant concern in estimating the parameters of equation 82; since there are only two explanatory variables in this equation, the second stage R_j^2 coefficient for either explanatory variable is equivalent to the r^2 value for the bivariate correlation between $\hat{X}_1$ and Z_3, and this value is only .16. In contrast, high multicollinearity is a

TABLE 2
Parameter Estimates for the Protest Violence Model
of Equations 80 Through 82

Explanatory Variable	Structural Parameter	Standardized Estimates of Parameters (with standard errors in parentheses)	
		2SLS	OLS
Equation 80			
X_2	β_{12}	1.54 (.51)	.36 (.07)
X_5	β_{15}	−.45 (.43)	.39 (.07)
Z_9	γ_{19}	−.05 (.13)	−.18 (.07)
Equation 81			
X_1	β_{21}	.75 (.27)	.41 (.08)
Z_3	γ_{23}	.10 (.08)	.13 (.07)
Z_4	γ_{24}	.08 (.10)	.14 (.08)
Z_6	γ_{26}	−.01 (.13)	.11 (.09)
Z_7	γ_{27}	−.02 (.09)	.03 (.08)
Z_8	γ_{28}	.02 (.10)	.09 (.08)
Equation 82			
X_1	β_{51}	.68 (.10)	.54 (.06)
Z_3	γ_{53}	.25 (.07)	.29 (.07)

problem in the second-stage regressions for estimating the parameters of equations 80 and 81. For equation 81, $R_1^2 = .85$, while for equation 80, R_2^2 equals .87 and $R_5^2 = .85$. While these R_j^2 values are not as large as the .98 (or greater) values characterizing some equations in the aspiration model, they are certainly large enough to warrant concern. Again, the best strategy would be to seek a larger data set by increasing the sample size above 126. A less appropriate strategy would be to delete one or more endogenous variables from the model, recognizing that while this will reduce the multicollinearity problem, it will simultaneously create specification error, thus generating additional bias in the 2SLS estimates. Kritzer weighed this trade-off and decided to delete X_5 from equation 80, and accept the consequences of the resulting specification error. Upon deletion of X_5, $\hat{\beta}_{12}^t$ drops from 1.54 to 1.05 while $\hat{\gamma}_{19}^t$ increases slightly in magnitude from –.05 to –.08. Note that the former is a sizable fluctuation. Indeed, it is not at all unusual to find substantial shifts in the values of parameter estimates when an explanatory variable is deleted from an equation characterized by high multicollinearity (Lewis-Beck, 1980: 60).

In contrast to Kritzer's choice, I would likely resist the temptation to delete variables from the protest violence model to overcome the multi-collinearity problem. Indeed, I believe that the deleterious consequences of specification error resulting from a deleted variable generally out-weigh those of multicollinearity in 2SLS. I think one is better off working with an accurately specified model, testing for multicollinear-ity in the second stage, and then reporting clearly the extent of the multicollinearity, than deliberately estimating a misspecified model. If multicollinearity is extensive for some equations, one must then exercise caution in interpreting the substantive meaning of the coefficient estimates for those equations, as the value of the estimates would vary considerably from one sample to another. Fortunately, the size of the standard errors for the parameter estimates of these equations and associated tests of significance give us information about how much caution we need exercise for a particular model. Multicollinearity is, at root, a problem of lack of sufficient data; and when the data are lacking, and no further data are available, we must basically accept that the data will yield parameter estimates with large standard errors, and glean as much information as we can from the estimates while recognizing their limitations.

6. CONCLUSION

We have seen that while all recursive models are identified, the strict assumptions made in such models (i.e., that the model is hierarchical, and thus characterized by a total lack of reciprocal causation among variables, and that there are mutually uncorrelated error terms) are unrealistic in many substantive social science contexts. When the assumptions of recursive models are not met, nonrecursive models must be used. With nonrecursive models, identification is not assured, and even when such models are identified, OLS regression—an estimation technique appropriate for estimating parameters of recursive models— is inappropriate; for nonrecursive models, OLS parameter estimates are both biased and inconsistent. Fortunately, given only the assumption that each error term in a model is uncorrelated with all exogenous variables in the model, many nonrecursive models can be identified through the use of zero restrictions. Furthermore, when a nonrecursive model is identified, and adequate data are available, alternatives to OLS regression are available which yield consistent estimates of the model's parameters; 2SLS is the most common of these techniques.

The topics examined in this paper should provide sufficient background for most social scientists who wish to employ nonrecursive models. There are, however, further topics relating to nonrecursive models which cannot be examined at length in this paper, but which do warrant attention. To complete this volume, a few of these general topics are outlined below.

Other Functional Forms

Our attention has been restricted in this paper to nonrecursive models containing structural equations that are *linear* and *additive* in nature. But just as the regression model can be modified to allow for various *nonlinear* (e.g., polynominal and exponential models), and *nonadditive*, or interactive, specifications (e.g., multiplicative models), so too can the structural equations within a nonrecursive model. For discussions of such specifications, see Tufte (1974: Chap. 3) and Hanushek and Jackson (1977: 96-108).

Lagged Endogenous Variables

Some social science theories, when accurately specified, generate models in which some of the explanatory variables in structural equations are prior values of the equations' dependent variables, i.e., lagged endogenous variables. For example, some models of budgetary politics view an agency's previous year's appropriation as an explanatory variable affecting the agency's current appropriation. The tests for identification and the estimation techniques presented in this paper can be easily adapted to accommodate lagged endogenous variables. A brief discussion of this topic is presented in Appendix 1.

Other Types of Identifying Restrictions

The algorithm presented in Chapter 3 and the strategy for modifying nonidentified nonrecursive models to achieve identification presented in Chapter 4 are limited in their applicability to models in which the only restrictions made to achieve identification are (1) zero restrictions (i.e., assumptions that certain parameters of the model are equal to zero) and (2) the assumption that each error term is uncorrelated with all exogenous variables in the model. While such restrictions are those most commonly used in the social sciences to identify nonrecursive models, a wide variety of other restrictions can be used. These include (1) an assumption that a pair of parameters in the model have a known ratio, (2) knowledge of the variances of some error terms in the model or the ratio of the variances for one or more pairs of error terms, and (3) an assumption that one or more pairs of error terms in the model are mutually uncorrelated. Appendix 2 contains a brief discussion of one type of model—block recursive models—which involve an assumption that certain pairs of error terms in the model are uncorrelated. But for more extensive discussions of alternative identifying restrictions, see Fisher (1966).

Alternative Estimation Techniques

This monograph presents only the common *limited-information* estimation techniques appropriate for nonrecursive models. Several *full-information* techniques are also available. As noted in Chapter 5, these full-information techniques generally yield more efficient estimators than the limited-information techniques. Thus, they can be particularly useful when multicollinearity results in 2SLS parameter estimates with large standard errors. Christ (1966) provides an extensive discussion of several of these full-information techniques.

Unobserved Variables

This paper assumes that the nonrecursive model under investigation contains variables all of which can be observed for a sample of cases, and measured without error. In many situations, however, these assumptions will not hold. For instance, one may be testing a theory that contains variables that cannot be observed at all. For example, the model of educational and occupational aspirations that Duncan et al. (1971) view as most complete, contains a variable—an adolescent's level of ambition— that the authors could not (at the time their research was conducted) measure.

In other situations, one may be able to measure all the variables in a theory, but some variables may necessarily be measured with error. This occurs because many of the variables in social science theories are abstract concepts, which cannot be observed directly (e.g., alienation, socioeconomic status, intelligence). Therefore, when measuring these concepts to test our theories, we are forced to rely on observable indicators of the concepts. If these indicators are merely substituted in the equations of a multiequation model, the variables will be measured with error—in violation of the model's assumption—and, depending on the type of measurement error, parameter estimates may be biased and inconsistent. A more appropriate specification of such a model would include both the unobservable abstract concepts and the observable indicators in a multiequation model explicitly identifying the causal linkages among the abstract concepts and between abstract concepts and their observable indicators.

When a multiequation model includes unobserved variables, the techniques presented in this paper can be used neither to test it for identification nor to estimate its parameters. But in some cases such models are identified,[38] and when they are identified it is possible to use a technique called LISREL to estimate parameters. In a sense, LISREL can be viewed as a powerful extension of *multiple-indicator models*—the subject of a paper in this series by Sullivan and Feldman (1979). For good discussions of LISREL (but ones that assume a knowledge of matrix algebra), refer to a volume edited by Goldberger and Duncan (1973; especially the article by Jöreskog) and Long's (1983) monograph.

APPENDIX 1

Lagged Endogenous Variables
in Nonrecursive Models

In Chapter 1, I noted that the term "exogenous variable" is used in this paper as a synonym for predetermined variable, since most predetermined variables used in social science research are exogenous. However, in some situations, it is reasonable to develop models in which lagged endogenous variables are treated as predetermined. In such situations, all statements made in this paper concerning exogenous variables apply to lagged endogenous variables as well. In particular, these lagged endogenous variables can be treated as if they were exogenous in applying the algorithm presented in Chapter 3.

However, lagged endogenous variables cannot reasonably be treated as predetermined variables in all situations. For example, consider a nonrecursive model containing a structural equation that has the endogenous variable $X_{i(t)}$ as the dependent variable on the right-hand side, and that includes the lagged endogenous variable $X_{i(t-1)}$ among the explanatory variables as in

$$X_{i(t)} = \gamma_{t,t-1} X_{i(t-1)} + \left(\sum_{j=2}^{k} \gamma_{ij} Z_j \right) + \left(\sum_{j=1}^{m} \beta_{ij} X_j \right) + \epsilon_{i(t)} \qquad [A1.1]$$

In order for $X_{i(t-1)}$ to be appropriately treated as predetermined, we must be able to assume that the error term in equation A1.1—$\epsilon_{i(t)}$—is uncorrelated with $X_{i(t-1)}$. What are the implications of this assumption?

To see the implications, consider the "implicit" structural equation having $X_{i(t-1)}$ as the dependent variable. Assuming the process generating $X_{i(t-1)}$ is the same as that generating $X_{i(t)}$, this implicit structural equation is

$$X_{i(t-1)} = \gamma_{t-1,t-2} X_{i(t-2)} + \left(\sum_{j=2}^{k} \gamma_{ij} Z_j \right) + \left(\sum_{j=1}^{m} \beta_{ij} X_j \right) + \epsilon_{i(t-1)} \qquad [A1.2]$$

where $\epsilon_{i(t-1)}$ is an error term assumed to reflect variables affecting $X_{i(t-1)}$ that are not explicitly included in the model. I claim that the assumption that $\epsilon_{i(t)}$ is uncorrelated with $X_{i(t-1)}$—which is necessary to reasonably treat $X_{i(t-1)}$ as a predetermined variable—is equivalent to the assumption that $\epsilon_{i(t)}$ is uncorrelated with $\epsilon_{i(t-1)}$, an assumption often referred to as that of a lack of *autocorrelation* (see Ostrom, 1980). To demonstrate the equivalence, we note that if $X_{i(t-1)}$ and $\epsilon_{i(t)}$ are uncorrelated, then $\epsilon_{i(t)}$ and $\epsilon_{i(t-1)}$ must be as well, since a nonzero correlation between $\epsilon_{i(t)}$ and $\epsilon_{i(t-1)}$ combined with the assumption that $\epsilon_{i(t-1)}$ is a cause of $X_{i(t-1)}$ would imply a nonzero correlation between $\epsilon_{i(t)}$ and $X_{i(t-1)}$. Also, it can be shown that a nonzero correlation between $\epsilon_{i(t)}$ and $\epsilon_{i(t-1)}$ ensures a lack of correlation between $X_{i(t-1)}$ and $\epsilon_{i(t)}$.

Thus, we have seen that for a lagged endogenous variable to be reasonably treated as a predetermined variable in a nonrecursive model, we must be willing to assume that there is no autocorrelation in the error term for the endogenous variable, the lagged value of which is included in the model. This is equivalent to assuming that the variables constituting the error term $\epsilon_{i(t)}$ affecting $X_{i(t)}$ are totally uncorrelated with the factors affecting the values of X_i during the previous time period, t-1. Clearly, in many substantive situations, this assumption will not be reasonable. Of course, if this assumption is not reasonable, it will be inappropriate to treat the lagged endogenous variable as a predetermined variable in the model.

When autocorrelation cannot be assumed absent, it is more reasonable to treat a lagged endogenous variable in a model as endogenous. Of course, in general, treating the variable as endogenous rather than predetermined tends to increase the likelihood that the model will be nonidentified. Furthermore, even if the model is identified, treating the lagged endogenous variable as strictly endogenous means that, when estimating the structural parameters using 2SLS,

84

an instrumental variable will have to be created for the lagged endogenous variable. Consequently, the chances for high multicollinearity in the second stage are likely to be greater. Despite the additional complications of treating a lagged endogenous variable as endogenous rather than predetermined, a lagged endogenous variable should not be treated as predetermined strictly for convenience. Only when one is confident that autocorrelation is not present should a lagged endogenous variable be treated as predetermined.

APPENDIX 2

Block Recursive Models

In the body of this paper, I restrict attention to nonrecursive models that make only the following assumptions about error terms: (1) that $\text{cov}(\epsilon_i, Z_j) = 0$ for all i and j, i.e., that each error term is uncorrelated with all exogenous variables in the model; and (2) that $E(\epsilon_i) = 0$ for all i, i.e., that all error terms have a mean of zero. If one is prepared to make a stronger set of assumptions about error terms by assuming in addition that certain pairs of error terms are mutually uncorrelated, the algorithm for testing for identification presented in Chapter 3 is not applicable without modification.

While the algorithm cannot, in general, be used with models assuming that error terms are mutually uncorrelated, it can easily be modified to deal with one such class of models often called *block recursive* models. In a sense, block recursive models share features of both recursive and nonrecursive models. Specifically, in block recursive models, the structural equations can be grouped into "blocks" (or subsets), so that while the model may be characterized by reciprocal causation among variables *within* the same block, there are strictly recursive relationships (unidirectional causality and mutually uncorrelated error terms) *between* blocks.

Consider the nonrecursive model depicted in Figure A2 and represented by the following equations:

$$X_1 = \beta_{12}X_2 + \gamma_{15}Z_5 + \epsilon_1 \qquad [A2.1]$$

$$X_2 = \beta_{21}X_1 + \gamma_{26}Z_6 + \epsilon_2 \qquad [A2.2]$$

$$X_3 = \beta_{31}X_1 + \beta_{34}X_4 + \gamma_{35}Z_5 + \epsilon_3 \qquad [A2.3]$$

$$X_4 = \beta_{42}X_2 + \beta_{43}X_3 + \gamma_{46}Z_6 + \epsilon_4 \qquad [A2.4]$$

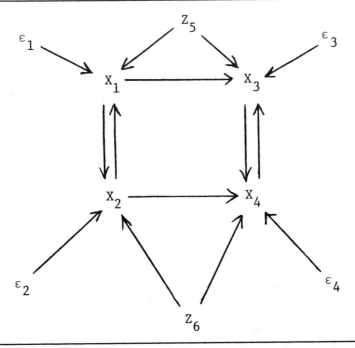

Figure A2: A Causal Diagram of the Nonrecursive Model of Equations A2.1 through A2.4

Given only the assumptions of the body of this paper (i.e., $E(\epsilon_i Z_j) = 0$ for all i and j, and $E(X_i) = E(Z_i) = E(\epsilon_i) = 0$ for all i), the reader may verify using the algorithm that equations A2.1 and A2.2 are exactly identified (for both these equations, R = 3 and m = 4), while equations A2.3 and A2.4 are underidentified (for both equations, $k_e < m_i - 1$). However, if we are prepared to make stronger assumptions about the error terms in the model, the model may be conceptualized as block recursive, and identification would be achieved. In particular, if we add the assumptions that ϵ_3 is uncorrelated with both ϵ_1 and ϵ_2, and that ϵ_4 is uncorrelated with both ϵ_1 and ϵ_2, the model becomes block recursive, with structural equations A2.1 and A2.2 constituting one block and equations A2.3 and A2.4 forming another block. With the additional assumptions, there is still reciprocal causation within the X_1–X_2 block and within the X_3–X_4 block, but there is a recursive relationship between the two blocks, as X_1 and X_2 are completely predetermined with respect to X_3 and X_4.

The algorithm presented in this article can be modified to be applicable with block recursive models. It is permissible to treat each block within the full model as a separate model and apply the algorithm to the equations within the block, ignoring all equations outside the block. But when counting exogenous and endogenous variables to determine m, k, m_i, and k_e for the equations in a particular block, any endogenous variable that appears in the block, but which is determined by a structural equation outside the block (i.e., any endogenous variable that does not appear on the left-hand side of a structural equation inside the block), must be treated as an exogenous variable. Then a sufficient condition for the identification of the full block recursive model is that the algorithm shows all equations in each block of the model to be identified within their blocks.

Using the modified algorithm, one may verify that the block recursive model of Figure A2 is identified. More specifically, for both equations in the X_1–X_2 block (i.e., equations A2.1 and A2.2), m = k = 2, R = 1 and, therefore, R = m – 1; thus, both equations are identified within the X_1–X_2 block. Furthermore, for both equations in the X_3 – X_4 block (i.e., equations A2.3 and A2.4), k = 4 (as X_1 and X_2 are now treated as exogenous variables along with Z_5 and Z_6), m = 2 (as X_3 and X_4 are counted as endogenous), and R = 1. Consequently, for both equations, R = m – 1; thus, equations A2.3 and A2.4 are identified within their block.

Again we have seen the importance of assumptions about error terms in determining whether or not a model is identified. The model of Figure A2 is not identified, given the assumptions in the body of this paper, but is identified if the additional assumptions required for a block recursive model are imposed. For this reason, one should exercise great caution when making an assumption that error terms in a model are uncorrelated; the assumption should not be made unless it is reasonable within the substantive context of the model.

APPENDIX 3

Matrix of Standard Deviations and Bivariate Product-Moment Correlation Coefficients for All Variables Used in Estimating the Parameters of the "Aspiration" Model of Equations 61 Through 64

	Original Variables[†]								Instrumental Variables[†]			
	X_1	X_2	X_3	X_4	Z_5	Z_6	Z_7	Z_8	$\hat{X}_1$	$\hat{X}_2$	$\hat{X}_3$	$\hat{X}_4$
X_1	12.631											
X_2	0.422	12.591										
X_3	0.625	0.328	12.445									
X_4	0.327	0.640	0.367	12.125								
Z_5	0.411	0.260	0.404	0.290	5.333							
Z_6	0.324	0.279	0.405	0.305	0.222	5.463						
Z_7	0.293	0.361	0.241	0.411	0.186	0.271	5.603					
Z_8	0.300	0.501	0.286	0.519	0.336	0.230	0.295	5.381				
$\hat{X}_1$	0.514	0.471	0.521	0.517	0.800	0.631	0.570	0.584	6.490			
$\hat{X}_2$	0.428	0.565	0.416	0.604	0.460	0.494	0.639	0.886	0.833	7.115		
$\hat{X}_3$	0.502	0.441	0.533	0.482	0.758	0.760	0.452	0.536	0.977	0.781	6.636	
$\hat{X}_4$	0.438	0.564	0.425	0.606	0.479	0.504	0.678	0.858	0.865	0.998	0.797	7.342

SOURCES: Correlations for original variables are from Duncan et al. (1971: 222); standard deviations for original variables from Hanushek and Jackson (1977: 280); instrumental variables constructed by author.

† Standard deviations are in diagonal entries; correlations are in off-diagonal entries; the mean of all variables is zero.

APPENDIX 4

Matrix of Bivariate Product-Moment Correlations for All Variables Used in Estimating the Parameters of the Protest Violence Model of Equations 80 Through 82

	Original Variables[†]								Instrumental Variables[†]	
	X_1	X_2	Z_3	Z_4	X_5	Z_6	Z_7	Z_8	Z_9	$\hat{X}_1$	$\hat{X}_2$
X_2	.61										
Z_3	.28	.33									
Z_4	.37	.39	.24								
X_5	.62	.51	.44	.56							
Z_6	.52	.42	.27	.16	.29						
Z_7	.39	.29	.09	.11	.17	.44					
Z_8	-.39	-.30	-.11	.01	-.26	-.29	.09				
Z_9	.41	.38	.18	.46	.40	.24	.24	-.03			
$\hat{X}_1$	.70	.60	.40	.53	.58	.74	.56	-.56	.58		
$\hat{X}_2$	.69	.62	.54	.63	.64	.68	.47	-.58	.61	.98	
$\hat{X}_5$	.58	.57	.63	.80	.70	.42	.24	-.37	.57	.83	.92

SOURCES: Correlations for original variables are from Kritzer (1977: 638); instrumental variables constructed by author.

† The mean of all variables is zero; the standard deviation of all variables is one.

APPENDIX 5
Glossary of Symbols

Symbol	Meaning
$\text{cov}(X, Y)$	population covariance of variables X and Y
$\text{var}(X)$	population variance of variable X
s_{XY}	sample covariance of variables X and Y
s_X	sample variance of variable X
$E(X)$	expected value (i.e., population mean) of variable X
$\hat{X}$	instrumental variable for X

NOTES

1. The literature on the factors determining individual's candidate preferences in an election is extensive. For substantive background in this area, see Goldberg (1966), Jackson (1975), and Page and Jones (1979).

2. For a discussion of the meaning of a "causal relationship," see Asher (1983: 8-13) or Blalock (1969).

3. I will adopt the typical custom in social science literature of using "causal diagrams" as a convenient device to represent hypotheses about causal relationships among variables. In such diagrams, an arrow is drawn from a variable X to a variable Y $(X \rightarrow Y)$ to represent the assertion that X is a cause of Y.

4. An *unbiased* estimator or a parameter is one that, on average, is equal to the true value of the parameter, i.e., the estimator $\hat{\Theta}$ is an unbiased estimator of Θ if $E(\hat{\Theta}) = \Theta$. See also Note 27, and refer to Wonnacott and Wonnacott (1979: 55-58) for a more detailed discussion.

5. The term "consistent" is used here in the traditional statistical sense. Loosely, $\hat{\Theta}$ is a consistent estimator of Θ if, as the sample size approaches infinity, the distribution of $\hat{\Theta}$ approaches a distribution with all probability concentrated at the point Θ. See Christ (1966: 263-264) for a more detailed discussion.

6. For an introduction to OLS regression analysis, see Lewis-Beck (1980). For discussions of recursive causal models, see Asher (1983: 30-48), or Duncan (1975: Chaps. 1-4).

7. While this is the traditional definition of a predetermined variable in the social science literature, a more precise definition would define a predetermined variable in a model as one that is assumed to be uncorrelated with all error terms in the model.

8. Indeed, one must exercise great caution when including lagged endogenous variables as predetermined variables in a nonrecursive model; see Appendix 1 for elaboration.

9. This paper will confine attention to linear additive models. (See Lewis-Beck [1980] for a discussion of the assumptions of linearity and additivity.) Also, for ease of presentation, I omit constant terms in the structural equations. However, constant terms can be subsumed under the notation of equation system 2, by setting one of the exogenous variables (e.g., Z_1) equal to one.

10. Indeed, if we also assume homoscedasticity, i.e., that the error terms in a recursive model have constant variance [$VAR(\epsilon_j) = \sigma_j^2$], the Gauss-Markov theorem ensures that coefficient estimators are BLUE (the Best Linear Unbiased Estimators), i.e., the estimators that have minimum variance among the class of linear unbiased estimators (see e.g., Wonnacott and Wonnacott, 1979: 21-28).

11. We also assume that all variables and error terms in the model have a mean value of zero. This assumption is merely to simplify presentation by adjusting the location of the origin of the measurement scales for variables to allow deletion of constant terms from the model's equations.

12. To simplify the analysis of the wheat market model, we have been assuming that the relationships between (1) D_t and P_t and (2) S_t and P_t are *deterministic*, i.e., that each value of P_t is associated with unique values of D_t and S_t. But we can also develop a *stochastic* model—more typical of the kind commonly analyzed in social science research—by adding error terms to equations 10' and 11' to give:

Demand Curve: $\quad Q_t = a_D + b_D P_t + \epsilon_D$
Supply Curve: $\quad Q_t = a_S + b_S P_t + \epsilon_S$

However, just as before, the equations in this market model are not identified. If this model were a true representation of the supply and demand forces at work in the market, observation of the quantity of wheat sold and the price of wheat over time would yield a cluster of points around the intersection of the true supply and demand curves, determined as the two curves shift randomly from their true positions by the amounts of their error term values for each time period:

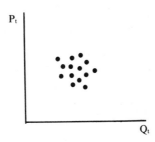

Given only this observed cluster of points, it is impossible to estimate accurately the parameters of the demand and supply curves.

13. See Appendix 2 for illustrations, but refer to Fisher (1966) for a detailed discussion of alternative types of restrictions that can be used to bring about the identification of an equation.

14. The concept "minimally sufficient" is admittedly vague. I will provide a more specific statement of the conditions necessary for an equation to be exactly identified and to be overidentified in the section entitled The Reduced-Form Perspective.

15. Since $U = \epsilon_1$, U is uncorrelated with Z_3 by the original assumptions of the model. Also, since Z_3 is assumed uncorrelated with ϵ_1 and ϵ_2, and since V is equal to ϵ_2 plus a constant (β_{21}) multiplied by ϵ_1, Z_3 is necessarily uncorrelated with V.

16. For a proof of these claims about linear combinations, see Christ (1966: 315-318), and Goldberger (1964: 312-313).

17. However, if not all the variables have a mean of zero, and thus constant terms are included in the equations, these terms can be ignored when testing for identification.

18. Readers familiar with matrix algebra can find more traditional (but equivalent) presentations of the rank condition in Wonnacott and Wonnacott (1979: Chap. 18) and Hanushek and Jackson (1977: 254-264).

19. If constant terms are included in the structural equations, these terms can be ignored in forming the system matrix.

20. I recognize that beginning with this step, the motivation behind some of the individual steps in the algorithm are not at all obvious. But a detailed discussion of the logic behind each separate step of the algorithm goes beyond the needs of most readers. The important point to remember is that when taken as an aggregate, the individual steps or procedures in the algorithm simulate the process of taking linear combinations of selected equations in a multiequation model.

21. Those familiar with matrix algebra may note that "simple form" is a synonym for "row reduced form," since asterisks represent numbers assumed to be different from zero.

22. Note that the reasonable parallel hypothesis—that for the respondent's friend as well, intelligence is a cause of aspiration—is not inconsistent with the model of Figure 11 as long as $cov(\epsilon_2, \epsilon_4)$ is not assumed equal to zero; if the hypothesis is true, friend's intelligence level is one of the factors reflected in the correlated error terms, ϵ_2 and ϵ_4.

23. This model was adapted from Duncan et al.'s research by Hanushek and Jackson (1977).

24. For this revised model, $m = k = 4$. For equations 61 and 62, $k_e = 2$, $m_i = 2$, and the algorithm reveals that $R = 3$. Thus, for both equations, $R = m - 1$ and $k_e > m_i - 1$. For equations 63 and 64, R also turns out to equal 3 and $k_e = 2$, but $m_i = 3$.

25. For the model, $m = 3$ and $k = 5$. For all three structural equations, $m_i = 3$ and $R = 2$. $k_e = 3$ for equations 66 and 67, but $k_e = 2$ for equation 65.

26. Note that while adding an exogenous variable to a model will never make a previously identified equation underidentified, it may make an exactly identified equation overidentified.

27. See Asher (1983: Appendix A) for a discussion of the meaning of "expectation" and a verification of the equivalence of covariances and variances to the expected values of products and squares of variables, respectively.

28. One estimator is defined as more efficient than another when its sampling distribution has smaller variance than the other's. See Wonnacott and Wonnacott (1979: 58-60) for more details.

29. See Christ (1966) for a detailed discussion of full-information estimation techniques.

30. For a more detailed discussion of this implication of perfect multicollinearity, see Lewis-Beck (1980: 58).

31. For general discussions of alternative strategies for dealing with high multicollinearity, see Lewis-Beck (1980: 58-63).

32. See Kritzer (1976) for a more detailed discussion of the multicollinearity problem in 2SLS and several illustrations of its effects.

33. Appendix 3 contains (1) the standard deviations of all variables in the aspiration data set along with (2) correlations between all pairs of variables.

34. $m = 3$ for the model, and for all structural equations, it turns out that $R = 2$. For equation 80, $k_e = 5$ and $m_i = 3$; for equation 81, $k_e = 1$ and $m_i = 2$; for equation 82, $k_e = 5$ and $m_i = 2$.

35. Most indicators for the variables in the protest violence model are scales based on several items in an "event questionnaire" (see Kritzer, 1977). Appendix 4 contains a correlation matrix for all variables employed in the analysis.

36. My 2SLS estimates differ slightly from those reported by Kritzer (1977), probably as a result of rounding errors in the correlation matrix used to reproduce Kritzer's analysis.

37. Kritzer (1976: 87) argues that a negative value for the coefficient β_{15} is "nonsensical." But I believe that the negative value is consistent with deterrence theories (e.g., Gamson, 1975), which would predict that arrests should discourage further violence by protestors.

38. As can be expected, whether or not a multiequation model with unobserved variables is heavily dependent on the nature of assumptions about error terms.

REFERENCES

ACHEN, C. H. (1977) "Measuring representation: perils of the correlation coefficient." American Journal of Political Science 4: 805-815.

ASHER, H. B. (1983) Causal Modeling. Beverly Hills, CA: Sage.

BLALOCK, H. M., JR. (1969) Theory Construction. Englewood Cliffs, NJ: Prentice-Hall.

———(1967) "Causal inference, closed populations, and measures of association." American Political Science Review 61: 130-136.

CHRIST, C. F. (1966) Econometric Models and Methods. New York: John Wiley.

DEEGAN, J. (1975) "The process of political development: an illustrative use of a technique for regression in the presence of multicollinearity." Sociological Methods and Research 3: 384-415.

DUNCAN, O. D. (1975) Introduction to Structural Equation Models. New York: Academic Press.

———(1966) "Path analysis: sociological examples." American Journal of Sociology 72: 1-16.

———A. O. HALLER, and A. PORTES (1971) "Peer influences on aspirations: a reinterpretation," pp. 219-244 in H. M. Blalock, Jr. (ed.) Causal Models in the Social Sciences. Chicago: Aldine-Atherton.

ERIKSON, R. S. (1976) "The influence of newspaper endorsements in presidential elections." American Journal of Political Science 20: 207-223.

FISHER, F. M. (1966) The Identification Problem in Econometrics. New York: McGraw-Hill.

GAMSON, W. A. (1975) The Strategy of Social Protest. New York: Dorsey Press.

GOLDBERG, A. E. (1966) "Discerning a causal pattern among data on voting behavior." American Political Science Review 60: 913-922.

GOLDBERGER, A. S. (1964) Econometric Theory. New York: John Wiley.

———and O. D. DUNCAN [eds.] (1973) Structural Equation Models in the Social Sciences. New York: Seminar Press.

HANUSHEK, E. A. and J. E. JACKSON (1977) Statistical Methods for Social Sciences. New York: Academic Press.

HIBBS, D. E., Jr. (1973) Mass Political Violence: A Cross-National Causal Analysis. New York: John Wiley.

HOERL, A. and R. KENNARD (1970) "Ridge regression: biased estimation for nonorthogonal problems." Technometrics 12: 55-67.

JACKSON, J. E. (1975) "Issues, party choices, and presidential votes." American Journal of Political Science 19: 161-185.

KLEIN, L. R. (1962) An Introduction to Econometrics. Englewood Cliffs, NJ: Prentice-Hall.

KRITZER, H. M. (1977) "Political protest and political violence: a nonrecursive causal model." Social Forces 55: 630-640.

94

——(1976) "Problems in the use of two stage least squares." Political Methodology 3: 71-93.

LAND, K. C. (1971) "Significant others, the self-reflexive act and the attitude formation process: a reinterpretation." American Sociological Review 36: 1085-1098.

——(1969) "Principles of path analysis," pp. 3-37 in E. F. Borgatta and G. W. Bohrnstedt (eds.) Sociological Methodology, San Francisco: Jossey-Bass.

LEMIEUX, P. (1978) "A note on the detection of multicollinearity." American Journal of Political Science 22: 183-186.

LEWIS-BECK, M. A. (1980) Applied Regression: An Introduction. Beverly Hills, CA: Sage.

LONG, J. S. (1983) Covariance Structure Models: An Introduction to LISREL. Beverly Hills, CA: Sage.

MASON, R. and A. N. HALTER (1968) "The application of a system of simultaneous equations to an innovation diffusion model." Social Forces 47:182-195.

NAMBOODIRI, N. K., L. E. CARTER, and H. M. BLALOCK, Jr. (1975) Applied Multivariate Analysis and Experimental Designs. New York: McGraw-Hill.

OSTROM, C. W. (1980) Time Series Analysis: Regression Techniques. Beverly Hills, CA: Sage.

PAGE, B. and C. JONES (1979) "Reciprocal effects of policy preferences, party loyalties and the vote." American Political Science Review 73: 1071-1089.

SULLIVAN, J. L. and S. FELDMAN (1979) Multiple Indicators: An Introduction. Beverly Hills, CA: Sage.

THEIL, H. (1971) Principles of Econometrics. New York: John Wiley.

TUFTE, E. R. (1974) Data Analysis for Politics and Policy. Englewood Cliffs, NJ: Prentice-Hall.

WAITE, L. J. and R. M. STOLZENBERG (1976) "Intended childbearing and labor force participation among young women: insights from nonrecursive models." American Sociological Review 41: 235-251.

WONNACOTT, R. J. and T. H. WONNACOTT (1979) Econometrics. New York: John Wiley.

ABOUT THE AUTHOR

WILLIAM D. BERRY is Professor of Political Science at Florida State University. He received his Ph.D. at the University of Minnesota, and taught previously at the University of Kentucky. His major substantive areas of interest are public policy, political economy, and state politics. He is coauthor of *Multiple Regression in Practice* and *Understanding United States Government Growth*. He has also published numerous substantive articles and papers about research methodology in such journals as *American Political Science Review*, *American Journal of Political Science*, and *Journal of Politics*.

Quantitative Applications in the Social Sciences

A SAGE UNIVERSITY PAPERS SERIES

SPECIAL OFFERS
(for **prepaid** orders only)

Order all 93 for $665.88 and save over $165.00
or
Order any 10 papers for $71.60 and save over $17.00

Orders under $30 must be prepaid. California residents add 7.25% sales tax. All prices subject to change without notice.

On prepaid orders, please add $2.00 handling charge.

SAGE PUBLICATIONS

1/93

Quantitative Applications
in the Social Sciences

(a Sage University Papers Series)

$8.95 each

SAGE PUBLICATIONS, INC.
P.O. BOX 5084
NEWBURY PARK, CALIFORNIA 91359—9924